HEALING AND HOPE

Healing and Hope

Messages to the Sick, the Suffering, and the Elderly

By

Pope John Paul II

ST. PAUL EDITIONS

Reprinted with permission from *L'Osservatore Romano*, English Edition.

Cover Photo: DSP

ISBN 0-8198-3317-7 cloth
0-8198-3318-5 paper

Printed in the U.S.A. by the Daughters of St. Paul
50 St. Paul's Ave., Boston, MA 02130

The Daughters of St. Paul are an international congregation of religious women serving the Church with the communications media.

CONTENTS

that eternal expression of the children of the earth. At the same moment was heard the voice of heaven, that "world" of God dwelling in the inaccessible tabernacle of glory. The majesty of the eternal God and mother Earth making herself known by the wail of the newborn Infant enable us to glimpse the prospect of a new peace, reconciliation, and covenant:

"To us is born the Savior of the world";
"All the ends of the earth have seen the salvation of our God."

2. Nevertheless, at this moment, at this strange hour, the ends of the earth are still afar off. They are pervaded by a period of waiting, far from peace. The hearts of people are filled rather with weariness; people have fallen asleep as have the shepherds in the Bethlehem valleys close by. What is happening in the stable, in the rock cave, has a dimension of profound intimacy: it is something between the Mother and the Babe to be born. No outside person has access. Even Joseph, the Nazareth carpenter, is but a silent witness. She alone is fully aware of her motherhood. She alone perceives the special expression of the Infant's wailing. The birth of Christ is preeminently her mystery, her great day. It is the feast of the Mother.

It is a strange feast: there is no trace of the synagogue liturgy, no reading of the prophets or singing of the Psalms. "Sacrifices and offerings you have not desired, but a body you have prepared for me" (Heb. 10:5) seems to be what is said by the wailing of the One who, although He is the eternal Son, the Word who is of one being with the Father, "God from God, Light from Light," has become flesh (Jn. 1:14). He reveals Himself in that body as one of us, a little Infant, in all His frailty and vulnerability. Dependent upon people's care, entrusted to their love, undefended. He wails, and the world does not hear Him; cannot hear Him. The newborn Infant's wail can only just be heard a few steps away.

3. And so, brothers and sisters crowding this Basilica, I beg you: let us try to be more present *there* than here. Not many days ago, I manifested the great desire I felt to be in the cave of the nativity, to celebrate in that very place the beginning of my pontificate. Since circumstances do not allow me to do that, finding myself here with all of you, I am endeavoring all the more to be there spiritually with you all, in order to crown this liturgy with the depth, the ardor, the authenticity of an intense inner feeling. The liturgy of Christmas night is rich with a special realism: the realism of the moment that we are renewing, and also the realism of the hearts that are reliving that moment. All of us in fact are deeply moved, although what we are celebrating happened some two thousand years ago.

In order to have a complete picture of the reality of that event, in order to penetrate more deeply still into the realism of that moment and the realism of human hearts, let us remember that the event occurred precisely in the way it did: in abandonment and extreme poverty, in the cave-stable outside the town, because people in the town refused to receive the Mother and

Joseph into any of their homes. Nowhere was there room. From the beginning, the world showed itself inhospitable towards the God who was to be born as man.

4. Now let us reflect briefly on the lasting meaning of this lack of hospitality on man's part towards God. All of us here wish it were different. We wish that everything within us men should be open to God born as a man. It is with this desire that we have come here!

On this night let us therefore think of all the human beings that fall victim to man's inhumanity, to cruelty, to the lack of any respect, to contempt for the objective rights of every human being. Let us think of those who are lonely, old or sick; of the homeless; those suffering from hunger; and those whose misery is the result of the exploitation and injustice of economic systems. Let us also think of those who on this night are not allowed to take part in the liturgy of God's birth and who have no priest to celebrate Mass. And let us give a thought also to those whose souls and consciences are tormented no less than their faith.

The stable at Bethlehem is the first place for solidarity with man: for one man's solidarity with another, and for all men's with all men, especially with those for whom there is "no room at the inn" (cf. Lk. 2:7), whose personal rights are refused recognition.

5. The newborn Infant is wailing.

Who hears the Baby's wail?

But heaven speaks for Him, and it is heaven that explains it with these words:

"Glory to God in the highest heaven, and peace to men who enjoy his favor" (Lk. 2:14).

Touched by the fact of the birth of Jesus, we must hear this cry from heaven.

That cry must reach all the ends of the earth, all men must hear it anew.

A Son is given to us.

Christ is born to us. Amen.

Take Heart!

On December 27, 1978, Pope John Paul II delivered an address, of which the following is an excerpt.

I now want to address an affectionate greeting to our sick sisters and brothers, present at this audience.

Thinking of you, and of all those who are ill, I see a deep and mysterious analogy between your situation and that of the newborn Jesus in the manger at Bethlehem: that Baby was a little, frail, weak being, in need of everything, depending on everyone: yet He was the Son of God, the eternal Word incarnate in time, the Savior of mankind, the Lord of history.

How often, beloved daughters and sons, you may have felt useless in your infirmity, a burden to your dear ones; you have experienced—we may well say so—the humiliation, so deeply human, of being obliged to need others in everything, of being almost at the mercy of others. Look at Jesus in the cave at Bethlehem, who assures you that it is the world which needs the immeasurable riches of your suffering for its purification and for its growth. Take heart! God loves you, because He sees in you the image of His Son suffering on earth! Your dear ones love you, because you are their flesh and blood! The Church loves you, because you enrich the treasure of the communion of saints! The Pope has a particular preference for you, because you are his most sensitive sons, and asks you for the help and the strength of your apparent weakness, of your prayers and your sacrifices!

Love and Respect for the Aged

About forty thousand people greeted the Pope when he came to the window of his study at noon on December 31, 1978, to recite the Angelus with them. Pope John Paul addressed them as follows.

Today is the last day of the year of the Lord 1978. We take leave of this year, thanking God for all the good we have received during the twelve months that have passed. We bid farewell to it, asking God for forgiveness for all the evil that, in the course of these twelve months, has been inscribed in human hearts, in the history of peoples, in the history of continents. We ask God for forgiveness for our sins, for our shortcomings and negligences. We pray to have the grace and the necessary strength to enter the new period of time, the new year, and, as the Apostle says, not to let ourselves be overcome by evil, but to overcome evil with good (cf. Rom. 12:21).

In the period of Christmas, our thoughts and our hearts are particularly directed to children.

And it is right, because the Child Jesus was born for us at Bethlehem.

Today, however, I would like these thoughts of ours, our hearts and, above all, our prayers, directed to the smallest and the youngest, to go to "the more elderly." I have in mind not so much those who are of middle age (in the prime of their physical strength), but rather those of advanced age—grandfathers, grandmothers: old people.

These persons are sometimes forsaken. They suffer because of their old age. They also suffer because of the various troubles that advanced age brings with it.

But their greatest suffering is when they do not find the due understanding and gratitude on the part of those from whom they are entitled to expect it.

Today, on the Sunday after Christmas, dedicated to the veneration of the Family of Nazareth, let us remember and meditate on the fourth divine commandment: "Honor your father and your mother." This commandment is of fundamental importance for the development of "relations between the generations" not only in the family, but also in the whole of society. Let us pray to God that these relations will develop in the spirit of the fourth commandment!

It is just to the oldest that we must look with respect ("honor!"); to them, families owe their existence, education and maintenance, which have often been paid for with hard work and much suffering.

They cannot be treated as if they were now useless. Even if they sometimes lack the strength to be able to carry out the simplest actions, they have, however, experience of life and the wisdom that the young often lack. Let us meditate on the words of Holy Scripture: "What an attractive thing is judgment in gray-haired men, and for the aged to possess good counsel! How attractive is wisdom in the aged, and understanding and counsel in honorable men! Rich experience is the crown of the aged, and their boast is the fear of the Lord" (Sir. 25:4-6).

Therefore, the Pope's thoughts and prayers go to you old people today. I hope that all those present are willingly in harmony with the Pope; I hope that above all the youngest are. Grandchildren love their grandfathers and their grandmothers, and keep them company better than others.

Thus let us conclude this year in the spirit of rapprochement of the generations, in the spirit of mutual understanding and love.

The Tenderness of Jesus

On January 3, 1979, Pope John Paul II gave an address of which the following is an excerpt.

Let a thought of good wishes for the new year now go also to all those who are suffering in body and in spirit.

Rest assured that the Pope is always beside you with his prayer and with his fatherly tenderness: with that tenderness that Jesus had for the many infirm persons who were presented to Him during His public life, and whom He comforted by curing them and by proclaiming the glad news of salvation (cf. Lk. 4:18).

May my special blessing be of comfort and support.

The Image of Christ in Suffering Childhood

On January 7, 1979, John Paul II went to the Roman hospital of Bambino Gesù (the Child Jesus) on the slopes of the Janiculum. At the end of his visit, which lasted for over two hours, the Pope delivered the following address.

Brothers and sisters,

Allow me now, concluding this pastoral visit to this Hospital of the Child Jesus, to address a few simple words of greeting and encouragement to all of you who work in this institute for the relief and cure of the little patients.

Let a cordial thought go in the first place to Mr. Commissioner and to the whole administrative and medical management for the indefatigable activity carried out, and for the future programs which they intend to implement in order to make this place of healing correspond more and more to modern medical requirements. Then I greet the doctors, the assistants, the sisters and children's nurses, in whom I like to see a reflection of the thaumaturgical figure of Christ, who dedicated such a large part of His ministry to curing the sick and relieving the afflicted.

And what shall I say to you, dear children, patients in this hospital? I will tell you that I came up here to the Janiculum especially for you: to see you, to express to you personally all my affection for you, and to bring comfort in your sufferings, due both to illness and to the fact of being separated from your parents and your home. I pray that you may recover quickly and thus find again the joy of living in the midst of the dear members of your family.

I wish to address a particularly affectionate greeting also and above all to you parents and relatives of the little patients. You are bearing the drama of the illness of your children and, with imploring eyes, are asking yourselves the reason for innocent pain. Rest assured that you are not alone or abandoned: you do not suffer in vain! Your suffering conforms you to Christ, who alone can give a meaning and value to every act of your life.

Finally, to all of you present here, who attend this hospital in one way or another and apply yourselves to works of mercy and spiritual and social welfare, I will recall the promise that the Lord Jesus made to those who seek Him in the sick: "I was sick and you visited me...as you did it to one of the least of these my brethren, you did it to me" (cf. Mt. 25:34-40).

Expressing to you warmly my appreciation of the service you render the little patients, I exhort you to continue your mission with Christian faith, which makes you perceive in the sick person the very image of God. At the same time, in the name of the Child Jesus, after whom this hospital is named, and in the name of the Blessed Virgin, invoked by you as *Salus infirmorum*, I impart to all my special apostolic blessing, which can also be extended to the members of your families who have remained at home.

"I See in You the Suffering Lord"

On January 26, 1979, Pope John Paul II delivered the following greeting to poor people of the "Los Minas" district in the suburbs of the Dominican capital, Santo Domingo.

Beloved sons and daughters of the "Los Minas" district,

From the first moment of the preparation of my journey to your country, I gave priority to a visit to this district of yours, in order to be able to meet you.

And I wanted to come here just because it is a poor area, in order that you might have the opportunity—I would say to which you have the best claim—of being with the Pope. He sees in you a more living presence of the Lord, who suffers in our neediest brothers, who continues to proclaim blessed the poor in spirit, those who suffer for justice and are pure in heart, who work for peace, have compassion, and keep their hope in Christ the Savior.

But on calling you to cultivate these spiritual and evangelical values, I wish to make you think of your dignity as men and children of God. I wish to encourage you to be rich in humanity, in love for the family, in solidarity with others. At the same time I exhort you to develop more and more the possibilities you have of obtaining a situation of greater human and Christian dignity.

But what I have to say does not end here. The sight of the reality in which you live must make so many people think of what can be done effectively to remedy your condition.

On behalf of these brothers of ours, I ask all those who can do so to help them to overcome their present situation, in order that, particularly with a better education, they may improve their minds and their hearts, and be architects of their own elevation and of a more advantageous integration in society.

With this urgent appeal to consciences, the Pope encourages your desires for advancement, and with great affection blesses you, your children and relatives, and all the inhabitants of the district.

The Pope Will Remember You

During his visit on January 29, 1979, to the children's hospital in Mexico City, Mexico, the Holy Father delivered the following short address.

Beloved children,

On coming to spend these moments in your midst, I wish to greet the directors of the center, all the sick boys and girls in this children's hospital, and all the children who are suffering in their homes, in any part of Mexico.

Sickness prevents you from playing with your friends; so another friend, the Pope, who thinks of you so often and prays for you, has desired to come and see you.

I also greet your parents, brothers, sisters, relatives and all those who are concerned about your health and care for you with such attention and affection.

I now call on you to recite a "Hail Mary" to the Virgin of Guadalupe for you, who meet pain and sickness so early in your lives.

Beloved children, the Pope will continue to remember you, and he takes with him your smiling greeting with open arms, leaving you his embrace and his blessing.

You Are God's Chosen Ones

In the course of his visit on January 30, 1979, to the "barrio Santa Cecilia," one of the poorest districts of Guadalajara, Mexico, the Holy Father spoke as follows.

Beloved brothers and sisters,

I keenly desired this meeting, inhabitants of the district of Santa Cecilia, because I feel solidarity with you and because, being poor, you are entitled to my particular concern.

I tell you the reason at once: the Pope loves you because you are God's favorites. He Himself, on founding His family, the Church, kept poor and needy humanity in mind. To redeem it, He sent precisely His Son, who was born poor and lived among the poor in order to make us rich with His poverty (cf. 2 Cor. 8:9).

As a consequence of this redemption, carried out in Him who became one of us, we are now no longer poor servants, we are sons, who can call God "Father" (cf. Gal. 4:4-6). We are no longer abandoned, since, if we are sons of God, we are also heirs to the goods He offers abundantly to those who love Him (cf. Mt. 11:28). Could we doubt that a father gives good things to his children? (cf. Mt. 7:7ff.) Jesus Himself, our Savior, waits for us in order to relieve us when we are weary (cf. Mt. 11:28). At the same time, He counts on our personal collaboration to make us more and more worthy, being the architects of our own human and moral elevation.

At the same time, faced with your overwhelming situation, I call with all my strength on those who have means and who feel they are Christians, to renew their minds and their hearts in order that, promoting greater justice and even giving something of their own, no one will lack proper food, clothing, housing, culture and work; all that gives dignity to the human person. The image of Christ on the cross, the price of the redemption of humanity, is a pressing appeal to spend our lives in putting ourselves at the service of the needy, in harmony with charity, which is generous and which does not sympathize with injustice, but with truth (cf. 1 Cor. 13:2ff.).

I bless you all, asking the Lord always to illuminate your hearts and your actions.

The Prayer of the Sick

The following is an excerpt from the address to about thirty thousand faithful gathered in St. Peter's Square on February 11, 1979, for the usual Sunday appointment for the recitation of the Angelus.

...Today I wish, above all, to speak to you of my meeting with the sick. This meeting will take place in St. Peter's Basilica this afternoon, while I still have in my mind and my heart all the meetings with the sick in Mexico, and in particular that one which took place in the Church of the Dominican Fathers at Oaxaca.

I am grateful to those who organized that meeting: to the priests, physicians, and hospital attendants. Due to them, I was able, on Mexican land, to approach so many sick persons, my brothers and sisters. I was able to lay my hand on their heads, I was able to speak a word of compassion, of comfort, and I was able to ask for their prayer.

I count a great deal on the prayer of the sick, on the intercession with God of those who are suffering. They are so near Christ! And I approach them, aware that Christ is present in them.

The suffering of one's neighbor, the suffering of another man, the same as oneself in everything, always causes a certain uneasiness, almost a sense of embarrassment, in those who are not suffering. A question arises instinctively: Why he, and not I? One cannot avoid this question which is the elementary expression of human solidarity. I think it was this fundamental solidarity that created medicine and the whole health service in its historical evolution up to our own days.

We must stop, then, in front of suffering, in front of suffering man, to rediscover this essential link between one's human "self" and his. We must stop before suffering man, to testify to him and, as far as possible, together with him, to the dignity of suffering, I would say, all the majesty of suffering. We must bow our heads before brothers or sisters who are weak and helpless, deprived of what has been granted to us to enjoy every day.

These are just some aspects of that great ordeal which costs man so much, but which purifies him at the same time, as it purifies the one who seeks solidarity with the other, with the suffering human "self."

Christ said: "I was sick and you visited me" (Mt. 25:36).

Let us pray today for all the sick persons whom I met on the ways of my journey in Mexico, and also for those, even more numerous, whom I was not able to meet; let us pray also for those who will take part today in the Mass in St. Peter's Basilica and for all those who are suffering, wherever they may be.

We are your debtors, beloved suffering brothers and sisters. The Pope is your debtor!

Pray for us!

My thought also goes to the sanctuary of Lourdes, for today is the anniversary of the first vision that St. Bernadette had. Moreover, as you already know, the next International Eucharistic

Congress will take place just there, in the year 1981, on the important subject: "Jesus Christ, bread broken for the salvation of the world."

So, I warmly recommend this initiative, too, to your prayers, while we all invoke the Blessed Virgin together.

Dignity and Majesty of the Suffering Man

On February 11, 1979, John Paul II concelebrated the Eucharistic liturgy in St. Peter's Basilica for a great many sick people. The Holy Father delivered the following homily.

Beloved brothers and sisters,

1. I greet all of you who are present here today. I greet you in a particularly cordial way and with great emotion. Precisely today, February 11, the day on which the liturgy of the Church recalls every year the apparition of our Lady at Lourdes, I greet you, who are accustomed to go on pilgrimage to that sanctuary, and you, who help sick pilgrims: priests, doctors, nurses, and members of the health, transportation, and welfare services. I thank you because you have filled St. Peter's Basilica today and honor the Pope with your presence, making him almost a participant in your annual pilgrimages to Lourdes, in your community, your prayer, your hope and also in all your personal renunciation and that mutual donation and sacrifice, which characterize your friendship and solidarity. This Basilica and St. Peter's Chair need your pres-

ence. This presence of yours is necessary for the whole Church, for the whole of mankind. The Pope is grateful, immensely grateful to you for this. In fact, today's meeting is certainly accompanied by the joy which springs from a living faith, but also by considerable effort and sacrifice.

PRAYER FOR AND WITH THE SICK

2. The Lord Jesus, in today's Gospel, meets a man who is seriously ill: a leper, who begs Him: "If you will, you can make me clean" (Mk. 1:41). And immediately afterwards, Jesus forbids him to spread the news of the miracle, that is, to speak of his cure. And although we know that "Jesus went about...preaching the gospel of the kingdom, and healing every disease and every infirmity" (Mt. 9:35), the restriction, the "reservation" of Christ with regard to the cure He had brought about, is significant. Perhaps there is here a distant anticipation of that "reservation," that caution with which the Church examines all supposed miraculous cures, for example, those that have taken place at Lourdes for over a hundred years. It is well known to what severe medical controls each of them is subjected.

The Church prays for the health of all the sick, of all the suffering, of all the incurables humanly condemned to irreversible infirmity. She prays *for* the sick and she prays *with* the sick. She is extremely grateful for every cure, even if it is partial and gradual. And at the same time, with her whole attitude she makes it understood—like Christ—every cure is something exceptional, that from the point of view of the divine "economy" of salvation it is an extraordinary and almost "supplementary" fact.

"BE AN IMITATOR"

3. This divine economy of salvation—as Christ revealed—is certainly manifested in the liberation of man from that evil, which "physical" suffering is. It is manifested even more, however, in the interior transformation of that evil, which spiritual suffering is, in "salvific" good, in the good that sanctifies the one who suffers and, through him, also others. And, therefore, the text of today's liturgy, on which we must dwell today above all, are not the words: "I will; be clean," but the words: "Be an imitator of me." It is Saint Paul who addresses the Corinthians with these words: "Be imitators of me, as I am of Christ" (1 Cor. 11:1). Earlier than he, Christ Himself had many times said: "Come and follow me" (cf. Mt. 8:22; 19:21; Mk. 2:14; Lk. 18:22; Jn. 21:22).

These words do not have the power to cure, they do not liberate from suffering. But they have a transforming power. They are a call to become a new man, to become particularly like to Christ, in order to find in this likeness, through grace, all the interior good in that which in itself is an evil, which makes one suffer, which limits, which perhaps humiliates or is embarrassing. Christ, who says to suffering man "come and follow me," is the same Christ who suffers: the Christ of Gethsemane, the scourged Christ, Christ crowned with thorns, Christ on the way of the cross, Christ on the cross.... It is the same Christ who drained the cup of human suffering "which the Father gave Him" (cf. Jn. 18:11). The same Christ, who assumed all the ills of the earthly human condition except sin, in order to draw from them salvific good: the good of redemption, the good of purification and reçonciliation with God, the good of grace.

If He says to each of you, dear brothers and sisters: "Come and follow me," He invites you and calls you to take part in the same transformation, in the same transmutation of the evil of suffering into salvific good: that of the redemption, of grace, purification, and conversion...for oneself and for others.

Just for this reason, St. Paul, who so passionately wished to imitate Christ, says in another place: "In my flesh I complete what is lacking in Christ's afflictions" (Col. 1:24).

Each of you can make these words the essence of your own life and vocation.

I wish you this transformation, which is "an interior miracle" even greater than the miracle of healing; this transformation, which corresponds to the normal way of God's economy of salvation as Jesus Christ presented it to us. I wish you this grace and I implore it on each of you, dear brothers and sisters.

PRESENCE OF JESUS

4. "I was sick," Jesus says of Himself, "and you visited me" (Mt. 25:36). According to the logic of the same economy of salvation, He, who identifies Himself with each suffering person, waits—in this man—for other men, who "come

to visit Him." He waits for the expression of human compassion, solidarity, kindness, love, patience, solicitude, in all their various forms. He waits for the expression of all that is noble, elevated in the human heart: "you visited me."

Jesus, who is present in our suffering neighbor, wishes to be present in every act of charity and service of ours, which is expressed also in every glass of water we give "in His name" (cf. Mk. 9:41). Jesus wants love, the solidarity of love, to grow from suffering and around suffering. He wants, that is, the sum of that good which is possible in our human world. A good that never passes away.

The Pope, who wishes to be a servant of this love, kisses the forehead and kisses the hands of all those who contribute to the presence of this love and to its growth in our world. He knows, in fact, and believes that he is kissing the hands and forehead of Christ Himself, who is mystically present in those who suffer and in those who, out of love, serve the suffering.

With this "spiritual kiss" of Christ, let us prepare, dear brothers and sisters, to celebrate and take part in this sacrifice, in which the sacrifice of each of you has had its place since time immemorial. And perhaps it is particularly opportune to recall that, according to the letter to the Hebrews, on celebrating this sacrifice and praying "*cum clamore valido*" (Heb. 5:7), Christ is heard by the Father:

Christ of our sufferings;
Christ of our sacrifices;
Christ of our Gethsemane;

Christ of our difficult transformations;
Christ of our faithful service to our neighbor;
Christ of our pilgrimages to Lourdes;
Christ of our community, today, in St. Peter's Basilica;
Christ our Redeemer;
Christ our brother! Amen.

Love the Crucified

The following is an excerpt from the Holy Father's address of March 24, 1979.

Jesus is first of all the support of our suffering.

Suffering is a reality that is terribly real and sometimes even atrocious and heartrending. Physical, moral, and spiritual pain torments poor mankind at all times. We must be grateful to science, technology, medicine, and social and civil organizations which try in all ways to eliminate or at least assuage suffering; but it always remains victorious and the defeat weighs on afflicted and helpless man. It almost seems, in fact, that to greater social progress there corresponds a moral decline, with the consequence of other sufferings, fears, and concerns.

Suffering is also a mysterious and overwhelming reality.

Well, we Christians, looking at the crucified Jesus, find the strength to accept this mystery. The Christian knows that, after original sin, human history has always been a risk. But he also knows that God Himself willed to enter our pangs, pass through the agony of the spirit and the torment of the body. Faith in Christ does not take away suffering, but illuminates it, raises it, purifies it, sublimates it and makes it efficacious for eternity.

In any pain of ours, moral or physical, let us look at the Crucified! Let the Crucified reign, clearly visible and venerated, in our houses. Only He can comfort and reassure us! Let us love the Crucified, as your great theologian and doctor of the Church, St. Alphonsus Liguori, desired.

Christ, Your Friend

On April 4, 1979, after the general audience, the Holy Father spoke as follows.

A special, affectionate thought to all of you sick people, in body or in spirit, who have come from various nations to visit the Pope.

What a significant, cordial and interesting meeting is this one, which takes place between those who represent suffering humanity and the Vicar on earth of Him who willed to be the "Man of sorrows" for the purpose of giving value, comfort and hope to the suffering of every human existence!

The present liturgical period leads us to consider Christ, who, in His agony in the garden of Gethsemane, accepted trouble, anguish and deep sadness (cf. Mk. 14:33). He prayed, He entrusted Himself completely to the will of the heavenly Father and had comfort and strength enough to drain the cup of sorrow *(ibid.,* 14:36).

Beloved sick people, keep your eyes fixed on Christ, your Friend, your Model, your Consoler! Following His example, you will obtain that your trouble will change into serenity, your anguish into hope, and your sadness into joy; your suffering will become purification and merit for your souls, as well as a precious contribution to the spiritual good of the Church (cf. Col. 1:24).

I willingly bless you, your dear ones, and all those who assist you lovingly.

The Work of the Redemption Is Accomplished in Suffering

On May 22, 1979, the Holy Father met a group of invalids of the "Pope John XXIII Association" from Rimini and their assistants, and also some representatives of the International Catholic Committee for the sightless, in front of the Lourdes grotto in the Vatican gardens. John Paul II delivered the following address.

Beloved sons,

Allow me to manifest to you, without circumlocutions or introductory periphrases, but with immediate spontaneity, the various feelings in my heart, at this meeting. It takes place in such a poetic setting of silence, peace, and prayer, during a limpid and serene evening in May, at the foot of the grotto of our Lady or, better, close to the heart of the Blessed Mother who looks at us and smiles to us from the grotto constructed in these Vatican gardens, in devout and perennial memory of that place, near the Pyrenees, where she appeared, last century, as a heavenly vision, a messenger of hope and love for suffering and sinful humanity!

LIKE A FAMILY

My first thought is of sincere satisfaction and deep gratitude for all those who have promoted and organized this meeting of ours. It could be defined a "family meeting," because we are all gathered round the Blessed Virgin for a simple, spontaneous and affectionate dialogue, as happens between children and their mother, who sees everything, even the deepest secrets; who understands everything, even the longest silences; who enlivens everything, even the most insignificant things.

Thanks to you all, for coming to visit the Pope. Thanks, again, for the delicate sentiments you harbor in your hearts for the Vicar of Christ and which you intend to manifest on this particular occasion. Thanks, finally, for your presence, which can be considered almost a "sacramental presence" of Christ! Yes, you are, in your wounded and painful flesh, the expression of Christ crucified, and as it were the prolongation of His passion, so that each of you can repeat with St. Paul: "In my flesh I complete what is lacking in Christ's afflictions for the sake of his body, that is, the church" (Col. 1:24); and again: "We suffer with him in order that we may also be glorified with him" (Rom. 8:17). Christ, therefore, chooses you, unites you and assimilates you to Himself with the irreplaceable, ineffable means of suffering, through which He imprints in you His painful image and continues to carry out the work of redemption.

VALUE OF PAIN

What, then, is the value of your suffering? You have not suffered or do not suffer in vain. Pain matures you in spirit, purifies you in heart, gives you a real sense of the world and of life, enriches you with goodness, patience and endurance, and—hearing the Lord's promise re-echo in your heart: "Blessed are those who mourn, for they shall be comforted" (Mt. 5:4)—gives you the sensation of deep peace, perfect joy, and happy hope. Succeed, therefore, in giving a Christian value to your suffering, succeed in sanctifying your suffering with constant and generous trust in Him who comforts and gives strength. I want you to know that you are not alone, or separated, or abandoned in your *Via Crucis;* beside you, each one of you, is the Blessed Virgin, who considers you her most beloved children: Mary, who "is a mother to us in the order of grace...from the consent which she loyally gave at the annunciation and which she sustained without wavering beneath the cross..." (LG 61-62), is close to you, because she greatly suffered with Jesus for the salvation of the world.

Look to her with full confidence and filial abandonment: she looks at you with a special glance; she smiles to you with motherly tenderness; she follows you with solicitous care!

May this sweet mother assist you and protect you always. We pray to her for you, that she may be close to you, comfort you, give you peace and lead to fulfillment in you—for the good of the Church, for the spread of the Gospel, for the peace of the world—that plan of grace and love which unites you more closely to Jesus Christ and configures you to Him. I am certain that you will pray for the Pope and offer your sufferings to the Lord also for him, won't you? In this way, our mutual cordial talk will continue beyond this very short space of time.

To all of you, finally, to your relatives, to the doctors and those who assist you and look after you continually and affectionately, I impart the apostolic blessing, as a forecast of abundant heavenly favors and a token of my fatherly benevolence.

CATHOLIC COMMITTEE FOR THE BLIND

Pope John Paul II then addressed in French the members of the International Catholic Committee for the Sightless as follows.

I wish to greet also the members of the International Catholic Committee for the Blind, who are preparing their eleventh international congress.

Dear friends, I know your efforts in the service of the blind, especially in the developing countries where life is even more difficult for them. Receive all my encouragement!

Certainly, nature revolts spontaneously before suffering and infirmity. Is it not necessary, moreover, to reject them in a way in order to succeed in transcending them, in living, in spite of them, as fully as possible? That is, in fact, the meaning of the social action of your committee.

But faith in the risen Christ opens to a deeper perspective. The *Exultet* of Easter tells us that He is "the light which knows no decline," *"qui nescit occasum"!* Seek this light of the soul. Through it, suffering united with that of our Lord and of the Virgin Mary at the foot of the cross opens the way to eternal life, for oneself and for others.

May your congress, for the third age, work according to this double inspiration. Help the blind to live fully on the human plane. Help them also to progress generously towards this spiritual light "which knows no decline," which can illuminate and warm all old age, in spite of its sorrows, up to the last moment. May the Virgin of Light, who must be invoked every day, guide you herself in your apostolate. Be assured of my prayer for you and for all the blind persons you represent, and receive my blessing.

The Cross Transfigures Human Suffering

On the evening of June 4, 1979, John Paul II gave the following brief address to the sick outside the Monastery of Jasna Gora in Poland.

My pilgrimage to Poland cannot go without a word to the sick, who are so close to my heart. I know, my dear friends, how in your letters to me you often write that you are offering for my intentions the heavy cross of your illness and suffering, that you are offering it for my mission as Pope. May the Lord reward you.

Every time I recite the morning, midday and evening Angelus, I feel, dear fellow countrymen, your special closeness to me. I unite myself spiritually with all of you. In a particular way I renew the spiritual unity that binds me to every person who is suffering, to everyone who is sick, to everyone confined to a hospital bed, to every invalid tied to a wheelchair, to every person who in one way or another is meeting his cross.

Dear brothers and sisters, every contact with you, no matter where it has taken place in the past or takes place today, has been a source of deep spiritual emotion for me. I have always felt how insufficient were the words that I could speak to you and with which I could express my human compassion. I have the same impression today also. I feel the same way always. But there remains the one dimension, the one reality in which human suffering is essentially transformed. This dimension, this reality, is *the cross of Christ.* On His cross the Son of God accomplished the redemption of the world. It is through this mystery that every cross placed on someone's shoulders acquires a dignity that is humanly inconceivable and becomes a sign of salvation for the person who carries it and also for others. "In my flesh I complete what is lacking in Christ's afflictions" (Col. 1:24), wrote St. Paul.

Therefore, uniting myself with all of you who are suffering throughout the land of Poland, in your homes, in the hospitals, the clinics, the dispensaries, the sanatoria—wherever you may be —I beg you to make use of the cross that has become a part of each one of you for salvation. I pray for you to have light and spiritual strength in your suffering, that you may not lose courage but may discover for yourselves the meaning of suffering and may be able to relieve others by prayer and sacrifice. And do not forget me and the whole of the Church, and the cause of the Gospel and of peace that I am serving by Christ's will. You who are weak and humanly incapable, be a source of strength for your brother and father who is at your side in prayer and heart.

"Behold, I am the handmaid of the Lord; let it be to me according to your word" (Lk. 1:38).

May these words that Mary is pronouncing by the lips of so many human beings be a light on your path for all of you.

May God reward you, dear brothers and sisters. And God reward all those who are looking after you. Through every manifestation of this care the Word becomes flesh (cf. Jn. 1:14). For Christ said: "As you did it to one of the least of these my brethren, you did it to me" (Mt. 25:40).

"Come to Me"

At the general audience on June 20, 1979, the Holy Father had special words for the sick.

And now my greeting is addressed to the dear sick, present at this audience.

Last Sunday, we celebrated the solemnity of the Body and Blood of the Lord, of Emmanuel, which means "God with us," present under the appearances of the bread and the wine. Christ, immutable in His feelings of tenderness and mercy, as He once did along the roads of Palestine, still today, from the silent but most eloquent presence of the consecrated Host, addresses to the multitudes and in particular to the sick and suffering the consoling words:

"Come to me, all who labor and are heavy laden, and I will give you rest" (Mt. 11:28).

Make this invitation your own. Accept it in your heart with my blessing.

Light and Comfort

On June 27, 1979, at the general audience in Saint Peter's Square, Pope John Paul addressed the sick as follows.

Beloved sick friends, I address a particularly affectionate greeting to you and I recall to you the words of St. Peter to the first Christians: "If when you do right and suffer for it you take it patiently, you have God's approval. For to this you have been called, because Christ also suffered for you, leaving you an example, that you should follow in his steps" (1 Pt. 2:21-22). They are words that are always relevant and always valid for you and for everyone! May they give you light and comfort. I bless you all willingly.

The Grace of Fortitude

On July 18, 1979, the Holy Father greeted the pilgrims. An excerpt of his address follows.

To you sick people present here and to all those suffering in their homes or in hospitals, I address a particular greeting, with a special thought for children who are hospitalized.

Be assured that the Pope is and will always be with you. He follows you with fatherly understanding and with tender affection and does not cease to raise prayers to obtain for you the grace of fortitude, which will make you overcome the difficulties and ordeals to which illness subjects you. Always remember that your pain, if associated with that of the suffering Christ, is not only not in vain, but is a privileged source of salvation for all men.

May the Lord shower on you the abundance of His heavenly favors to sustain and comfort your hearts.

"God Chooses the Weak..."

On July 25, 1979, Pope John Paul addressed the crowds gathered for the general audience. The following is an excerpt.

"An embrace for you, dear sick people." I wish to remind you that "God chose what is weak in the world to shame the strong" (1 Cor. 1:27).

Before the reality of pain, Christian faith offers a Presence: the presence of One who suffered and died on the cross, and then was victorious, rising from the dead.

His victory is ours too, and through Him we have a hope of life and resurrection which does not fail us. Take heart. May the Lord assist you with His grace and His comfort. May my blessing sustain you.

The Pope Is One with You

On August 8, 1979, Pope John Paul II addressed a special word to the sick present at the general audience.

To you sick people present at this audience, and to all those who are afflicted and suffering in body and in spirit, my fatherly and grateful thought!

The Pope, the common Father of all, knows that no one can be surprised if he looks at you, beloved sick people, with predilection and special regard.

"Likeness to Christ"

The following is an excerpt from the Holy Father's address of August 22, 1979.

You, dear sick people, know that you have a privileged place in the heart of the Pope. How could you not be the object of special care, you who have within the Church the singular role of humbly accepting suffering which, precisely for that reason, is transformed into charity for all the brothers?

While I gratefully publicly note this witness of yours, I invite you, in likeness to Christ, to continue to make of your physical and moral sufferings, a chalice of propitiation and intercession. May my paternal blessing be a comfort to you and to your respective families.

"The Way of the Cross"

The following is an excerpt from the Holy Father's address of August 29, 1979.

My dear sick ones,

I wish to greet you also, and in a special way, with particular affection and emotion, because of your suffering and of your example of patience and courage.

I am very moved to be able to recall for you something which John Paul I said to a Cardinal, who after his election had offered him a book containing designs of the *Via Crucis:* "The path of the Popes is marked by the cross. Help this poor Christ to carry the cross, help the Pope to climb Calvary for the good of the Church, of souls and of humanity."

These are serious and anguished words, which I wish to recall to you, my dear sick ones, so that you may offer your prayers and your sufferings for the Pope and for his mission of Father and Pastor.

Know that I, in the name of the Lord, am always near to you with my prayers and my blessing.

"Bear the Marks of Christ"

On October 10, 1979, the Pope gave a talk of which the following is an excerpt.

To you sick people, who bear in your body and in your spirit the marks of Christ (cf. Gal. 6:17), there goes, in a quite special way, my fatherly, affectionate word of blessing.

I thank you for your precious presence, which offers to the eyes of all of us a deeply felt testimony of Christian fortitude, courage and faith. These are virtues that sustain you in the hard trials to which you have mysteriously been called and, at the same time, make others reflect on the real meaning of this earthly life, so frail and fleeting, and so incomprehensible without a superior faith.

You are, therefore, the benefactors of mankind. May the Lord reward you and console you in your sorrow.

"Value of Your Sacrifice"

In the course of the general audience on October 31, 1979, the Holy Father delivered an address of which the following is an excerpt.

I wish to assure you all, sick people, that I am particularly close to you with my heart and my prayer, aware of the value of your sacrifice which, while it elevates and strengthens your spirits, is a source of such grace for the whole Church. As the month of the rosary ends today, I am happy to call upon you to draw inspiration, joy and comfort from this prayer so dear to Christian tradition. Turn your eyes incessantly to the Blessed Virgin; she, who is the Mother of Sorrows and also the Mother of Consolation, can understand you completely and help you. Looking to her, praying to her, you will obtain that your tedium will become serenity, your anguish change into hope and your grief into love. I accompany you with my blessing, which I willingly extend to all those who assist you.

"Always Be Close to Jesus"

At the general audience in St. Peter's Square on November 7, 1979, John Paul II addressed the faithful. An excerpt from the address follows.

Beloved sick! The Pope, as he repeats continually at these meetings and at extraordinary ones, is close to you with his constant memory, his understanding, his affection and his prayer. I know how much you need to know that you are not alone in your suffering. Well, I tell you from my heart and with all humility: never lose heart; always be close to Jesus, with Jesus. He, first and foremost, is the Man of sorrows and of all human sufferings. He comforts you with the presence of His grace, and repeats to you with His example that you are precious collaborators of the Church because, as He makes her fruitful with His sacrifice, so you obtain with your sufferings mercy and particular gifts of assistance and protection.

May the apostolic blessing descend on you, on your dear ones, and on all those who look after you, to their common comfort.

Increase in Love

On November 14, 1979, the Holy Father addressed the following words to the sick.

I now wish to address a thought, by now a usual one, but always new and cordial, to the sick present at this audience.

Dear friends, the Pope looks to you with sincere predilection. He has a particular regard for you and reserves for you a special memory in his prayers, in order that you may always be serene in infirmity, fervent in spirit and pleasing to the Lord! I exhort you, furthermore, never to consider yourselves unlucky, disabled and useless. Though subject to the experience of suffering, which is often accompanied by loneliness, discouragement and inactivity, you must experience the fact that illness, when accepted and lived in a Christian way, elevates and ennobles you. In fact—according to the Apostle—suffering produces endurance, and endurance produces character, and character produces hope, and hope does not disappoint and contributes to an increase of love of God in your hearts (cf. Rom. 5:3).

May these thoughts, which I accompany with my fatherly blessing, always be a reason for hope and comfort for you.

"Special Presence of the Lord"

The following is an excerpt of the Holy Father's address of November 21, 1979.

I address a particularly affectionate and respectful thought to the sick. How could I not feel sincere and fatherly affection for those who, in any family or institute, perhaps in solitude, are sorely tried by painful physical and spiritual afflictions? But my greeting to you, dear sick people, besides being affectionate, is also respectful, because you are, among us, a special presence of the Lord. You possess a particular likeness to Christ the Redeemer; you have an extraordinary mission of salvation and sanctification, for yourselves and others.

May the Lord comfort you with the riches of His grace; may He free you, if it is His will, from your tribulations; may He give you serenity and courage, and so much faith and so much hope. My blessing, a very cordial one, to you.

"Have a Sense of Expectation"

On December 5, 1979, the Holy Father held the usual weekly audience in the Hall of Paul VI. The following is an excerpt of his address.

Beloved sick people,

The period of Advent, which we have started, prepares us for holy Christmas and, according to the spirit of the liturgy, makes us live mystically the sense of waiting for the Savior, which permeates the whole of the Old Testament.

If expectation is a typical characteristic of every Christian, you particularly, dear sick people, must have the sense of expectation! Nothing is lost of your suffering, which is united with Christ, the Redeemer of mankind.

This is the message of Advent, which I exhort you to meditate upon and live, while I accompany you with my affectionate blessing.

Concern for Those Who Suffer

On December 23, 1979, the Holy Father went to the Holy Spirit Hospital in Rome for a long visit to the sick. In the course of the visit, John Paul II delivered the following address.

Beloved brothers and sons of the Holy Spirit Hospital!

If the journey I had to make to come among you was a short and swift one, all the more intense and affectionate is the greeting that I wish to address to you at the moment when I meet you for the first time.

To you, illustrious members of the Board of Directors; to you, Mons. Fiorenzo Angelini, who carry out so solicitously the task of spiritual assistance in the hospitals and clinics of the city; to you, skilled doctors, nursing and clerical staff; to you, zealous chaplains and worthy sisters, who carry out your appreciated activity here in various ways and, in particular, to you dear sick people: I wish to extend to all, in the gentle, spiritual atmosphere of Christmas, the typical Christian greeting: "Blessed be the name of the

Lord!" Yes, it is precisely by glorifying Christ, that is, exalting and thanking Him who came among us as Savior; it is precisely by considering and meditating on the work He carried out for the whole of mankind and for every single man, that we find again the real roots of our deep unity and realize more clearly the reasons for which we are and feel and call ourselves brothers.

HISTORY OF THE HOSPITAL

1. Coming to this hospital, I cannot but recall the extraordinary and centuries-old history that has taken place in it. Coming into being as a place of meeting and reception for Saxon pilgrims (the *gens Saxonum)* who came to Rome, the country of faith, from the early Middle Ages—like so many other pilgrims of the various "nations" of Christian Europe—to venerate the memory of the Apostles, the original Holy Spirit hospice very soon qualified itself as an efficient and providential institution, becoming a place of prayer, assistance and care. Already its nearness to St. Peter's tomb conferred on it a privileged position; then its successive development and adaptation to the growing requirements not only of pilgrims, but also of the citizens of Rome, turned it into a large hospital, approved and protected by the Sovereign Pontiffs, who endowed it with the necessary goods so that it could carry out its activity, and in various ways—also through the collaboration of personal representatives and of commendatory abbots—gave it thoughtful attention.

But the mere mention of this significant historical function is sufficient. It seems to me more important, in fact, to point out a constant connotation: here Christian charity "has always been at home" in the course of the centuries; here works of mercy have expressed it in daily practice; here both have recorded a consoling, uninterrupted and exemplary operation. How many Holy Spirit Hospitals came into being in imitation of this main hospital? There was one even in my Krakow. Their operation assumed, certainly, different forms according to circumstances, but it always maintained the character of a preferential service to help the sick, the needy and the poor. And this not just in the recent past....

CONTROL CENTER TODAY

2. Coming to this hospital, I think, in fact, also of what the Holy Spirit Hospital is nowadays, that is, of its present function as "control center" in the hospital system of Rome. It presents a well-articulated structure in the variety of its wards, its laboratories and its nosological divisions. This structure not only helps, but coordinates and stimulates the activity of the other hospitals of the city.

There depends on it, in fact, the hospital administration of Rome, under the name of Pious Institute of the Holy Spirit, to which are entrusted the general management, the organization of care and decisions in these matters. Nor can I forget that there exists here a rich medical library, named after the great Giovanni Maria

Lancisi, as well as the famous academy of the same name, and that there is also attached the Historical Museum of Medical Art. In a word, "Holy Spirit," in the light of what it has been in the past and still is, offers an eloquent picture of high scientific qualification and the consequent capacity of meeting very well modern therapeutic, diagnostic and clinical requirements, in accordance with a tradition that has brought the Roman Medical School such distinction and renown before the world.

CONCERN FOR THE SICK

3. Coming to this hospital, I am thinking above all of my sick brothers, for whom it is institutionally destined. Yes, I am thinking of you, beloved sick, who are, unfortunately, obliged to be here in these days. They are days of holy joy, and they must be so also for you, in spite of your illness. I have come to bring to you brothers, tried in body and in the spirit, the immutable Word of the Gospel: a word of consolation, confidence and solidarity and—if you allow me—of special affection. You know my predilection for all the suffering, and this is an attitude which corresponds to the fundamental and primary duty of him who, succeeding Peter in the Roman See, has the formidable title of "Vicar of Christ." How could I represent Christ, if I forgot His constant concern for the sick, His exertions for them, the great words of faith addressed to them, His wonderful interventions, of which the pages of the Gospel are full? We read that the deaf and the blind, the crippled and the lame, paralytics and

lepers flocked to Jesus from every part of Palestine, "for power came forth from him and healed them all" (Lk. 6:19; cf. Mk. 1:32-34). How could I forget that "moral identification," which Jesus established between Himself and the suffering, and inserts as a criterion of judgment—a demanding and severe judgment—in that code which will regulate our "status" for eternity? "I was sick and you visited me(...). And when did we see you sick...? As you did it to one of the least of these my brethren, you did it to me" (Mt. 25:36, 39-40).

Having before my eyes those examples and this directive of the Lord, it is natural that I should look to you, feel you close and address to you the words of Jesus Himself: "Take heart, my son; your sins are forgiven"; "take heart, daughter; your faith has made you well" (Mt. 9:2, 22). Christ lives and is hidden in your persons, as His own sufferings live again and continue in yours, so that that value, which we derive from Christ's blood, continues and increases by means of your own pain, according to what St. Paul tells us: "In my flesh I complete what is lacking in Christ's afflictions for the sake of his body, that is, the church" (Col. 1:24; cf. 2 Cor. 1:5; 12:9). Here, brothers, is the point of arrival: your suffering is not sterile, it is not a plant that is wasted on the desert air, it is not blind and inexplicable cruelty. The Gospel, in fact, explains it and interprets it: pain is direct participation in Christ's redeeming sacrifice and, as such, it has a precious function in the life of the Church. It is a mysterious but real treasure for all the faithful by virtue of that circulation of grace, which Christ the Head diffuses to His Mystical Body and which the members of this Body exchange with one another.

I trust that these reminders will have the power to awaken in you, dear brothers, renewed spiritual energies, which will also be beneficial—I firmly hope—for the desired recovery of your physical health.

BETHLEHEM TO CALVARY

4. Coming to this hospital, I am thinking, finally, of Christmas which is imminent. Speaking of suffering just now, our glance arrived at the cross and Calvary; but before, there was Bethlehem with its cradle, with its stable. It was here that Christ the Man began His work, destined for universal salvation: a beginning which contrasts strangely with His identity as the true Son of God. Oh! What an admirable lesson the birth of Jesus the Savior offers us! If He, the Son of God, became Man "for us men and for our salvation," taking the ways of humility and charity, how can we insist on attitudes of pride and selfishness? A Christian Christmas, to be a true celebration of the nativity of Jesus, must be inspired by its same virtues and must open us to sentiments of peace and understanding, brotherhood and charity towards our fellowman.

SERVICE OF LOVING CARE

In this fervent vigil, in this place of hope and pain, my visit does not wish to be only a sign of good wishes for the sick, in order that their recovery may be hastened, but also the occasion to urge all those who, both on the therapeutic and on the spiritual plane, look after them. Oh! The treatment of diseases and care for the sick are really transformed when we are permeated with those virtues and those sentiments that Christmas teaches us. Professional service really becomes, then, attentive, sensitive and specific care for the individual person of the brother suffering in *that* bed, in *that* ward. For this reason, my visit concludes with the prayer that the Spirit of Jesus the Savior will pour those heavenly gifts on each of you, the sick and nurses, assistants and professors, chaplains and sisters. In this way the forthcoming festivity will be for you all a source of consoling serenity and holy joy.

"Gift of Your Prayers"

The following is an excerpt from the address of the Holy Father, delivered to a general audience on January 2, 1980.

I wish to greet particularly the young disabled persons of Vibo Valenzia. To them and to all the sick I address a word of encouragement, comfort and Christian certainty. The Word of God experienced in His human nature also suffering and even death. The Incarnation is a great light which is reflected on the dramatic problem of human pain, a problem that is always alive and relevant. Beloved ones, who are united with the sufferings of Christ, we ask you today for the gift of your prayer for us, for the Church, for mankind; and for the gift of your hope, rooted in the resurrection of Christ.

Bethlehem: Light that Illumines

The following is an excerpt of an address delivered by John Paul II on January 6, 1980.

Let my particularly affectionate greeting reach you, too, beloved sick people who have wished to take part in this audience.

Especially for you, infirm and suffering, Jesus, the divine Word who became incarnate in Bethlehem, is the Light that illuminates you and guides you in acceptance of your illness, in hope of cure, in the certainty that your sufferings will become joy and eternal glory for heaven.

Like the Wise Men, who came from faraway to worship the divine Child, bring your precious gifts: the gold of your sorrow, the incense of your faith, the myrrh of your patience.

"Blessed Are Those Who Mourn"

The following is an excerpt from a talk given by Pope John Paul II on January 21, 1980.

To you, beloved sick people present at this audience, and to all those suffering in body or in spirit, I address my grateful thought together with an affectionate greeting. As you well know,

Jesus Christ looked with special love on the infirm, the afflicted, the poor, the handicapped and the suffering, reserving for them the most tender love of His Heart, the greatest miracles of His power and the assurance of a special place in His kingdom: "Blessed are those who mourn, for they shall be comforted!" (Mt. 5:4) This thought must comfort you in tribulation, it must stimulate you to offer your suffering to the Lord, and make you undertake to suffer with Christ in order to purify and sanctify your souls and, at the same time, to contribute to the good of the holy Church (cf. Col. 1:24).

I willingly bless you, your dear ones, and all those who assist you lovingly.

"You Resemble Christ"

The following excerpt is from the address delivered by John Paul II on January 23, 1980.

I greet with special affection the sick and anyone afflicted by tribulations in body or in soul. You, dear sick people, are, among us and in the world, a special presence of the Lord; you resemble Christ the Redeemer in an extraordinary way; to you is entrusted a mission of salvation, for yourselves and for others.

May the Lord comfort you with the abundance of His grace; may He free you from your sufferings if it is His will; may He give you serene courage and much faith. For this purpose the Pope prays for you too and imparts his blessing.

"Always Look Up"

The following is an excerpt of the address during the general audience on January 30, 1980.

...You sick people, however, are no less dear to me. God certainly looks upon you with special affection, because you resemble more His Son, in the pain and humiliation of the cross. I realize how hard your lives are, and how you may sometimes be overcome by dismay. But I exhort you, with a fatherly heart, always to look up to where light and grace come from. And, furthermore, the Church is purified every day by your sufferings united with those of the Lord. With these sentiments I am so close to you, always, and I bless you.

Bear Witness to the Power of Christ's Cross

Over fifteen thousand sick were gathered in prayer around the Holy Father on February 11, 1980, for a Eucharistic Celebration on the occasion of the anniversary of the apparition of the Virgin in the Grotto at Lourdes. During the Liturgy of the Word, John Paul II delivered the following homily.

Venerated brothers and beloved sons and daughters!

1. It is with heartfelt emotion and deep joy that I address my cordial greeting this evening to the Cardinal Vicar, in the first place, and to the other Cardinals present; to my venerated brothers in the episcopate, to priests of the secular and

regular clergy, and in particular to those who concelebrate with me this Eucharist, which sees us gathered around the altar of Christ, to remember the wonder of grace operated in her whom we confidently invoke as powerful advocate and sweet Mother.

My greeting is then addressed to the sisters, present in considerable numbers on this occasion also; and further to the persons who belong, in various capacities, to the different Marian associations, as also to all those who have been drawn to this celebration by their devotion to the Blessed Virgin.

I want to reserve a special word of greeting to the sick, who are the guests of honor at this meeting: at the cost of considerable sacrifices they have wished to be present this evening to bear witness in person to the love that binds them to the heavenly Mother, to whose shrine in Lourdes many of them have certainly already gone on pilgrimage: you are welcome among us, together with those who are doing their utmost to assist you.

My greeting, therefore, is extended to all those gathered in this patriarchal basilica of St. Peter which receives such an exceptional visit today. I want to express my gratitude to all. Beloved sons, I feel indebted to you all. It is thanks to you, in fact, that the particular reality which bears the name of Lourdes is transferred to this basilica today. A reality of faith, hope and charity. A reality of sanctified and sanctifying suffering. The reality of the presence of the Mother of God in the mystery of Christ and of His

Church on earth: a presence that is particularly alive in that elect part of the Church which is constituted by the sick and the suffering.

DRAWN TO LOURDES

2. Why is it precisely the sick who go on pilgrimage to Lourdes? Why—we wonder—has that place become for them almost a "Cana of Galilee," to which they feel invited particularly? What draws them to Lourdes with such power?

The answer must be sought in the Word of God, which is offered to us by the liturgy in the holy Mass which we are celebrating. At Cana there was a wedding feast, a feast of joy because it was a feast of love. We can easily imagine the "climate" that reigned in the room of the banquet. Also that joy, however, like every other human reality, was a joy that was threatened. The bride and bridegroom did not know it, but their feast was about to be transformed into a little drama, owing to the fact that they had run out of wine. And that, if we stop to think about it, was only the sign of so many other risks to which their love, which was beginning, would be exposed subsequently.

Luckily for them, "the mother of Jesus was there" and consequently "Jesus also was invited to the marriage" (cf. Jn. 2:1-2), who, requested by His Mother, miraculously changed the water into wine. The banquet was able to continue joyfully, and the bridegroom received the compliments of the steward of the feast (cf. Jn. 2:9-10), surprised by the quality of the last wine served.

The banquet of Cana, beloved brothers and sisters, speaks to us of another banquet: that of life, at which we all desire to sit down to taste a little joy. The human heart is made for joy and we must not be surprised if each of us strains towards this goal. But reality, unfortunately, subjects so many persons to the experience of grief, often a tormenting one: illnesses, bereavements, misfortunes, hereditary taints, loneliness, physical torture, moral anguish—a range of concrete "human cases," each of which has a name, a face, a history.

These persons, if they are animated by faith, turn to Lourdes. Why? Because they know that as at Cana, "the mother of Jesus is there": and where she is, her Son cannot fail to be. This is the certainty that moves the multitudes who pour into Lourdes every year in search of relief, comfort and hope. Sick people of every kind go on pilgrimage to Lourdes, supported by the hope that, by means of Mary, Christ's salvific power will be manifested in them. And, in fact, this power is always revealed with the gift of immense serenity and resignation, sometimes with an improvement of the general conditions of health, or even with the grace of complete cure, as the numerous "cases" that have taken place in the course of over a hundred years bear witness.

DISCOVERING THE VALUE OF SUFFERING

3. The miraculous cure remains, however, in spite of everything, an exceptional event.

Christ's salvific power, propitiated by the intercession of His Mother, is revealed at Lourdes particularly in the spiritual sphere. It is in the hearts of the sick that Mary makes the thaumaturgic voice of her Son heard: a voice that dissolves miraculously the stiffening of bitterness and rebellion, and restores eyes to the soul to see the world, others, and one's own destiny in a new light.

The sick discover at Lourdes the inestimable value of their own suffering. In the light of faith they arrive at seeing the fundamental significance that pain may have, not only in their own lives, interiorly renewed by this flame which consummates and transforms, but also in the life of the Church, the Mystical Body of Christ. The Blessed Virgin, who took part personally in her Son's passion, standing courageously beside His cross (cf. Jn. 19:25), is able to convince more and more souls to unite their own sufferings with Christ's sacrifice, in a choral "offertory" which, crossing time and space, embraces the whole of humanity and saves it.

Aware of this, on the day when the liturgy recalls the Lourdes apparitions, we wish to thank all the willing souls who, suffering and praying, collaborate so effectively for the salvation of the world.

May our Lady be beside them, as she was beside the bride and bridegroom at Cana, and see to it that the generous wine of love will never be absent in their hearts. Love, in fact, can work the miracle of causing the fragrant rose of joy to bloom on the thorny stem of suffering.

CALLING ON MARY

4. But I do not want to forget the servants of Cana, who played an important part in the working of Jesus' miracle by carrying out His orders with docility. Lourdes, in fact, is also a miracle of generosity, altruism and service, beginning with Bernadette, who was the very special instrument to transmit to the world the Virgin's evangelical message, to discover the spring of miraculous water, and to ask for the construction of the "chapel." Above all, she was able to pray and sacrifice herself, withdrawing into the silence of a life completely dedicated to God. And how could we forget, then, the immense host of persons who, inspired by the humble shepherd girl, have dedicated themselves, and dedicate themselves, with extraordinary love to the service of the shrine, to the carrying out of the services, and especially to care of the sick? Therefore my thought, our thought, of appreciation and gratitude now goes to all those who are doing everything they can beside you, beloved sick persons, surrounding you with their thoughtful attentions: the doctors, the auxiliary medical personnel, all those who carry out the necessary services, both during the pilgrimages and in the places where you are usually hospitalized, and above all to the members of your families, on whom the greatest effort of assistance weighs.

Like the servants of Cana, who—unlike the steward of the feast—"knew" about the miracle worked by Jesus (cf. Jn. 2:9), may those who assist you always be aware of the miracle of grace that is accomplished in your lives and help you to be equal to the task that has been entrusted to you by God.

THOSE WHO SERVE OTHERS

5. Beloved sisters and brothers, gathered around the altar we now continue the celebration of the Eucharist. Christ is with us: this certainty diffuses immense peace and deep joy in our hearts. We know that we can rely on Him who is everywhere, now and always. He is the Friend who understands us and supports us in dark moments, because He is "a man of sorrows, and acquainted with grief" (Is. 53:3). He is the traveling companion who restores warmth to our hearts, enlightening them about the treasures of wisdom contained in the Scriptures (cf. Lk. 24:32). He is the living bread that has come down from heaven, who can light in this mortal flesh of ours the spark of life that does not die (cf. Jn. 6:51).

Let us continue on our way, therefore, with renewed energy. The Blessed Virgin indicates the way to us. Like the bright morning star, she shines before the eyes of our faith "as a sign of sure hope and solace, until the day of the Lord shall come" (LG 68). Pilgrims in this "vale of tears," we sigh to her: "Show us after this our exile, Jesus, the blessed fruit of your womb, O clement, O pious, O sweet Virgin Mary!"

Suffering: "Lasting Claim to Merit"

The following is an excerpt of the Holy Father's address delivered on February 13, 1980.

My thought now goes to the sick people who honor the audience this morning with their presence. Beloved sons, the Pope esteems you highly and thanks you for the very important contribution that each of you makes, with his own suffering, to the life of the Church. Take heart: suffering passes but the fact of having suffered remains as a lasting claim to merit before God and man. May my apostolic blessing comfort you.

"A Word of Encouragement and Consolation"

The following is an excerpt from an address given by the Holy Father on March 5, 1980.

Let a word of encouragement and consolation now go to all you sick people, who, with your painful, but exceedingly precious suffering, enrich the Church with merits and special graces. In fact, illness suffered for the Lord and offered to Him becomes not only for you, but also for the whole Mystical Body, a very special opportunity for expiation, purification, propitiation and spiritual elevation.

In this period of Lent, you who are nearest to the "man of sorrows, and acquainted with grief," as Christ was described by the prophet Isaiah (53:3), succeed in giving this purpose to your pain, in order to be able to face it with fortitude, and also with joy, as the Apostle Paul exclaims: "With all our affliction, I am overjoyed" (2 Cor. 7:4).

In confirmation of these wishes may my special blessing descend in abundance on you and on all those who assist you lovingly.

"Put on the Lord Jesus"

The following is an excerpt of the Holy Father's address of March 12, 1980.

Let a special word of greeting now go to all of you, sick brothers present here.

Beloved in Christ, in this period of Lent try to make your own St. Paul's call to "put on the Lord Jesus Christ" (Rom. 13:14) and to "become like him in his sufferings and death" (Phil. 3:10), living in your flesh the reality of pain, following the example of the suffering Jesus, as a sure way to the joy of resurrection. Endeavor, therefore, to carry out this vocation of yours generously, basing it on deep Christian faith and on ardent love for Christ. May my blessing accompany you and those who assist you lovingly in your daily offering.

Absolute Faithfulness

The following is an excerpt of the Holy Father's address given on March 19, 1980.

To the beloved sick, present here, and to all those suffering in body and in spirit, I wish to address my cordial greeting, which I accompany with fatherly wishes and with the assurance of a remembrance in prayer.

The feast of St. Joseph gives me the opportunity to exhort you to turn your eyes to him, a just and pious man, to learn the great lessons of absolute faithfulness to the Lord, to beg for the necessary energy to overcome with courage and merit the adversities of life and to obtain always his powerful and sweet protection.

With the smile of the holy patriarch, may my blessing accompany you!

"Look to the Crucifix"

On March 26, 1980, the Holy Father addressed the sick as follows.

Let my most heartfelt and affectionate greeting reach you, as always.

While, unfortunately, there is so much violence in present-day society, I turn to you especially, so that in these holy days which bring us nearer to Easter you will look to the crucifix in order to cooperate with more intense love in the redemption of mankind, according to the mysterious but always wise designs of Providence.

May my blessing accompany you.

Source of Serenity and Hope

The following is an excerpt of the Holy Father's discourse on April 9, 1980.

Also to the sick who are taking part in this audience I would like to offer the comfort of a precious word, that of the Apostle Paul. The latter, after a long experience of tribulations of every kind, writing to the Christian community of Rome, confides to them this conviction of his: "I consider that the sufferings of this present time are not worth comparing with the glory that is to be revealed to us" (Rom. 8:18). Take heart, beloved sons: I remember you in prayer, in order that Christ, who died and rose again, may be for you a source of serenity and hope, light and fortitude, merit and sanctification. As a token of that, I give you my special blessing.

In the Cross, God Changed the Meaning of Suffering

On April 13, 1980, the Holy Father visited the "Little House of Divine Providence," the center founded by St. Joseph Benedict Cottolengo. Before beginning the visit to the center, John Paul II met in the church a large group of sick people, men and women religious, nurses and voluntary personnel and delivered the following address.

Beloved brothers and sisters in Christ Jesus!

It is with deep emotion that I speak to you in this place, sacred to human suffering. What suffering is not present here? Between these walls, which arose from the great heart of St. Joseph Benedict Cottolengo, human suffering in its thousand aspects and Christian love in its varied expressions have met, and from this meeting there has come forth what popular wisdom has defined as the "citadel of miracles." I greet warmly all its inhabitants.

1. "Cottolengo" is a name which—in Italy and everywhere—now has the value of a very high witness: that of the Gospel, living and lived to its extreme consequences. Christ's words: "As you did it to one of the least of these brethren, you did it to me" (Mt. 25:40), were accepted by the founder of the "Little House" as a concrete and challenging program, on which to base his life. What must have struck Cottolengo above all in Christ's words was that reference to "the least of these brethren," that is, to those rejected by everyone. Only those who take into account the words of St. Paul, which Cottolengo chose as the motto of his work: "*Caritas Christi urget nos*" ("The charity of Christ urges us on"), can succeed in divining something of the miracles of love, inexplicable on the human plane, which have been carried out and are carried out every day in the humble and reserved concealment of the "Little House."

Love is the explanation of everything. A love that opens to the other in his unrepeatable individuality and says to him the decisive words: "I want you to be here." If one does not begin from this acceptance of the other, however he may present himself, recognizing in him a true, even if dimmed, image of Christ, one cannot say that one really loves. Cottolengo understood this. Cafasso, Don Bosco, and Don Murialdo understood it. All the saints in the Church were formed on this fundamental lesson.

All real love reproduces in a certain measure God's original evaluation, repeating with the Creator, with regard to every concrete human individual, that his existence is "very good" (Gn. 1:31). How could we fail to recall, in this connection, the stress that St. Paul lays on the universal dimension of charity? He states that he has made himself a slave to all (cf. 1 Cor. 9:19), that he has become "all things to all men" *(ibid.,* 9:22), that he tries "to please all men in everything he does" *(ibid.,* 10:33); and he exhorts: "as we have opportunity, let us do good to all men" (Gal. 6:10).

No discrimination, therefore. The parable of the "good Samaritan" is significant: and Cottolengo commented on it with his life. As a good "laborer of Providence," as he liked to call himself, he did not make plans arranged beforehand, but tried to meet on each occasion what circumstances proposed to him "by chance" (cf. Lk. 10:31). The result is this great undertaking, in which the evangelical "comment," which he started, continues to be enriched with new developments thanks to the generous dedication of so many souls, who were inspired by his example and are still inspired today.

COMPLETE DETACHMENT

2. But the complete availability to the demands of love with regard to man's sufferings, which Cottolengo provided during his life, was not the fruit of a vague sentimentalism. It was based on an attitude of radical poverty, that is, of full detachment from himself and his own property, which made possible an unreserved openness to the challenges of God's grace and to those of human misery. The whole secret lies here.

Cottolengo, and in this he was no different from your other Turinese saints, had learned this secret in the school of Christ. Was it not Jesus, in fact, who was the first to give us the example of extreme self-privation, He who "though he was rich, yet for our sake became poor, so that by his poverty we might become rich" (cf. 2 Cor. 8:9)? Christ carried the gift of Himself to the peak of His sacrifice on the cross (cf. Phil. 2:5ff.), and He did so "while we were yet sinners" (Rom. 5:8). On Calvary we are offered an absolute testimony of what it means "to be for" others, in loving obedience to God's will.

The Christian's charity has a model by which it can constantly measure itself; in it, it has also the source from which to draw the necessary energy in order to express itself with ever-renewed enthusiasm. Before Christ who "did not please himself" (Rom. 15:3), but "gave himself for our sins" (Gal. 1:4), the Christian learns not to "look only to his own interests, but also to the interests of others" (Phil. 2:4); he learns to take his eyes off himself to look at the other. Thus he arrives, for the first time perhaps, at becoming fully aware of the existence of the other with his problems, his needs and his solitude.

It is this interior poverty that frees us from ourselves and makes us available for the appeals that our neighbor makes to us at every moment. This is the point: it is necessary to descend to this depth to grasp the heart of the charitable action of a Don Bosco, a Murialdo and, in particular, of St. Joseph Benedict Cottolengo. Only if we view things from this standpoint can we understand the "logic" of that complete abandonment of his to Providence, which has become proverbial. He who has detached himself from everything, has also given up calculations about what he has or does not have, when it is a question of meeting his neighbor's needs. He is perfectly free, because he is completely poor. And it is precisely in such poverty, in which the limits placed by the "prudence of the flesh" have disappeared, that God's power can be manifested even in the free gratuitousness of the miracle.

THE GREAT MIRACLE

3. Numerous prodigious episodes are narrated in Cottolengo's life. But the great miracle, which for more than a century and a half continues to be manifested in this "House" in the normality of everyday life, is that of so many human beings who choose to take their place at the side of brothers and sisters on whom illness has set its seal and to share with them their own life.

Human suffering is a continent of which none of us can claim to have reached the boundaries. But walking through the wards of this "Little House," one explores it in such a way that is more than sufficient to have an idea of its impressive proportions. And the question presents itself: why?

Let us hearken once more, in this unique setting, to the answer of faith: the life of historical man, defiled by sin, is lived, in fact, under the sign of Christ's cross. *In the cross, God has changed radically the meaning of suffering.* The latter, which was the fruit and testimony of sin, has now become participation in Christ's redemptive expiation. As such, it contains within it, already now, the announcement of the definitive victory over sin and its consequences, by means of participation in the glorious resurrection of the Savior.

A few days ago, with the liturgy leading us by the hand, we lived again the dramatic moments of the passion and death of the Lord, and we listened again to the triumphal Alleluia of His resurrection. The Paschal Mystery, then, contains the definitive word on human suffering. Jesus assumes the pain of each one in the mystery of His passion and transforms it into a regenerating power for the one who is suffering and for the whole of mankind, in the perspective of the ultimate triumph of the resurrection, when "through Jesus, God will bring to life with him those who have fallen asleep" (1 Thes. 4:14).

REDEEMING VALUE

4. In the light of the risen Christ, I address, therefore, the sick people who are patients in this House, and, in them, all those who bear on their shoulders the heavy cross of suffering. Beloved brothers and sisters, take heart! You have a very noble task to carry out: you are called to "complete in your flesh what is lacking in Christ's afflictions for the sake of his body, that is, the church" (cf. Col. 1:24). With your suffering you can strengthen faltering souls, bring back to the right path those who have gone astray, restore serenity and confidence to those in doubt and anguish. Your sufferings, if generously accepted and offered

in union with those of the crucified Christ, can make an outstanding contribution in the struggle for the victory over the forces of evil, which threaten modern humanity in so many ways.

In you Christ prolongs His redeeming passion. With Him, if you so wish, you can save the world!

I wish to reserve a special word also for the men and women religious who, following in the steps of Cottolengo, are living their consecration to Christ in complete dedication of themselves to the sick, gathered here and elsewhere. Remain faithful to the charism of your founder. Be guided, like him, by an enlightened and deep faith, that will keep you in constant touch with Him who stretches out His imploring hand to you in every suffering person. Seek in prayer the source of a charity that "bears all things, believes all things, hopes all things, endures all things" (1 Cor. 13:7). Remember Cottolengo's maxim: "Prayer is our first and most important task," because "prayer makes the Little House live." What you do is certainly a service to society, to the civil community, in short to man; but it is also, and essentially, a witness to the perennial vitality of the Gospel, and to that "faith working through love" (Gal. 5:6). If your effort should lack this supernatural dimension, the "Cottolengo" would cease to exist.

I wish to address a word of esteem and appreciation also to the medical and nursing personnel, who are carrying out their delicate work with competence and a sense of responsibility in the various departments of the House. Continue to work with a spirit of dedication and brotherly charity, aware that you are rendering a service which goes beyond mere professional limits and reaches the dignity of a real and proper mission.

I address a special greeting and a word of encouragement to the young, who offer their service free of charge in the wards of the "Little House." Beloved friends, in a world in which many people of your age indulge in the facile promptings of the consumer society, or pursue the illusory mirages of the fashion of the moment, or let themselves be swept away by the dark fascination of violence, you cry out with the silent witness of your example that life is beautiful and has a value only if lived responsibly in the service of brothers, in an attitude of respect, trust and love. It is a fundamental message. Continue to proclaim it courageously today, tomorrow, always. God is with you.

A SIGN OF GOD'S LOVING PRESENCE

A word of deserved recognition, finally, to the citizens of Turin, whose generosity Providence has now been using for many years to work miracles of kindness for so many sorely-tried brothers. The "Little House" is a particularly eloquent sign of God's loving presence in the fabric of our human history. Today Turin is a city shaken by dramatic social tensions and too frequent explosions of violence. The fact that this "sign" of Christian brotherhood continues to exist in it, is a motive that induces us not to despair for the future. In spite of the threatening clouds of hatred, which darken the horizon, love will eventually lead back to the ways of understanding and respectful and harmonious collaboration.

With this wish, and invoking the motherly assistance of the Blessed Virgin, whom the evangelist presents to us standing by her Son's cross (cf. Jn. 19:25), courageous in solidarity with His suffering for us, I impart to you all, with extraordinary intensity of affection, my apostolic blessing, as a propitiation of spiritual consolation and a token of the Lord's eternal reward.

"Unite Your Sufferings to Jesus"

The following is an excerpt from the general audience address of April 16, 1980.

I cannot forget my beloved sick brothers, to whom, interpreting the sentiments of all those taking part in this meeting, I wish to offer a word of encouragement and Christian certainty.

At this moment I remind you, who bear in your hearts and your bodies the signs of the passion, of the words addressed by Jesus to the disciples who were going to Emmaus, discouraged and depressed by the tragic end of their Master: "Was it not necessary that the Christ should suffer these things and enter into his glory?" (Lk. 24:26) This statement casts a powerful light not only on the human vicissitudes of Jesus, but also on the lives of you all, who are marked by the stigmata of illness.

Unite your sufferings with those of Jesus; offer them as a pure sacrifice to the Holy Trinity for the good of the Church and mankind. While we all entrust ourselves to your prayers, we also say "thank you" with emotion for your continual testimony of faith and hope.

Unite with the Suffering Jesus

The following is an excerpt from an address the Holy Father delivered to the faithful gathered in St. Peter's Square for the general audience on April 30, 1980.

I dedicate a special word of greeting and comfort to all the sick present here, and for their consideration at the beginning of the month of May, I would like to offer the image of the Virgin at the foot of the cross.

"Standing by the cross of Jesus was his mother" (Jn. 19:25). The Virgin, with her mother's grief, participated in a quite particular way in the passion of Jesus, cooperating deeply in the salvation of mankind. Like Mary, each of us can and must unite with the suffering Jesus in order to become, with his own pain, an active part in the redemption of the world, which He effected in the Paschal Mystery.

With these wishes, may my comforting blessing, strengthened by Mary's motherly help, accompany you and those who lovingly assist you in your daily offering.

Great Mystery of Solidarity in Suffering

On May 12, 1980, the Holy Father met with the lepers of the leprosarium of Adzope. It was his last engagement in Africa, and perhaps the most moving. He visited the "Raoul Folloreau" National Institute for leprosy founded in 1971. After greeting all the patients suffering from the disease, and also the medical and religious staff, he spoke to them as follows.

Dear friends,

1. I come to pay you a visit, and in the first place to greet you, one and all, with respect, with affection.

It is the Bishop of Rome who comes to you, that is, the spiritual head of the Catholic community of Rome. But he has at the same time the task of being the center of unity among Christians of the whole world, of being their pastor, like the shepherds of flocks who do not forget any lamb. In this leper hospital, not all are Catholics; I respect their religious sentiments, their way of addressing God, according to their conscience. For no one is dispensed from turning towards God; and how can we forget Him in times of affliction? But I think I have a good word for everyone. For Christ Jesus, the Son of God, whom I serve and represent among you, stopped with predilection before human suffering, disease, infirmity, and above all, infirmity, such as leprosy, which sets one somewhat apart from others, thus creating a double suffering.

Certainly, He came for everyone, in order that everyone, big and small, rich and poor, the just and sinners, may know that the kingdom of God was open to them, that the love of God was upon them, that the life of God was destined for them, by means of faith and conversion. The Pope also addresses the whole people and, if he meets especially the spiritual and civil leaders, it is because their responsibilities are wider, for the good of a large number. But I should fail in my mission if I did not pass considerable time with those that Jesus loved particularly, because of their misery, because they needed comfort, relief, cure and hope. So I wanted my last visit in Africa to be for you. And through you, I visit in spirit and embrace all the other lepers and sick people of this country, and of the whole of Africa.

2. Thanks to medicine, thanks to the zeal of admirable pioneers, thanks to the daily dedication of numerous men and women nurses, of friends of every kind who help you, among whom there are many religious, thanks also to the civil leaders who have promoted the assumption of this responsibility, it has been possible to improve your fate; not only your health, but your environment, often permitting you to live, as it were, in a village, as if in a family. Now leprosy is no longer so frightening as before, especially if it is detected and treated quite early. I join you in thanking all these friends of lepers, who dedicate their lives to you. Without knowing it, perhaps, or without believing it, they are doing exactly what Christ asked. May God sustain them and reward them!

3. But I am sure too that they receive consolation from you. Not only because you love them, but because they admire your patience, your serenity, your courage, the solidarity that unites you, the family sense that you maintain. For you are not just in the care of others: you take charge of yourselves, you do everything you can to live, to walk, to work, with poor means, with the handicapped limbs that the disease leaves you. This hope is beautiful. I am moved by it myself. This desire to live pleases God, and I hope that you will develop it. You are, it could be said, your own doctors.

4. But I do not come just to give you this human encouragement. I come to confirm what priests, sisters and Christian laity have probably said to you already: in your misery, God loves you. This disease does not correspond to His plan of love. And you yourselves are in no way to blame. Do not look upon it as a fatality. Look upon it just as a trial. The Christ we worship Himself underwent a trial, that of the cross, a trial that disfigured Him, and without any fault of His own. He put Himself in the hands of God, His Father. He turned towards Him to ask for deliverance too. But He accepted; He offered. And His suffering became for countless men, for you, for me, a cause of salvation, forgiveness, grace and life.

This solidarity in suffering is a great mystery. It is the heart of our religion. Those who are Christians understand my language. Your suffering, accepted, borne with patience and love of others, offered to God, becomes a source of grace, for you for whom the Lord has His paradise in store, and for many others. You can also pray for me, and for all those who entrust their misery to me.

May God help you! May God give you peace!

5. I now turn towards those among you who have opened their souls to faith in Jesus Christ the Savior and who are going to receive Baptism and Confirmation, after long preparation. What a grace! They are going to become visibly members of the family of Christians, the Church. After renouncing the devil and his allurements and proclaiming their faith, they, too, are going to receive, like us, the forgiveness of their sins, the life of Christ, in order to participate in His sacrifice and His resurrection. Love of God will be spread in their hearts by the Holy Spirit. They will be able to receive as nourishment the holy bread that is the body of Christ. God, the Father, Son and Holy Spirit, will dwell in them. They will become in their turn witnesses to Christ's love for their suffering brothers.

God bless you, dear sons and daughters! May He bless all the inhabitants of this leper hospital! May He bless all your brothers who are suffering from leprosy as well as their families, their friends and those who assist them!

Eternal Values of the Spirit

The following is an excerpt from a talk given by the Holy Father at the general audience of May 14, 1980.

I now address, with special fatherly affection, the group of participants in the Plenary Assembly of the Committee for the European Area of the *International Federation of the Blind*, who have come here from various countries to express to the Pope the homage of their devotion.

I receive you very willingly, beloved sightless brothers and sisters, and I thank you for this presence, which is a testimony of Christian faith. I know very well what noble sentiments distinguish you and with what dignity you bear your sufferings. I know also of the Christian faithfulness which inspires your life and your actions, instilling in you peace and serenity. May your interior fortitude be a source of light and inspiration for those who have eyes to see, but often do not see because they are unable to go beyond material appearances. The Church is grateful to you for the strength and example with which you are able to suffer and irradiate the eternal values of the spirit which put us into communion with God.

As a sign of my special benevolence I impart to you the apostolic blessing, which I extend to all those who accompany you and assist you.

CONFIDENCE AND ENCOURAGEMENT

To the sick, and in particular to those who come from "Cottolengo," Turin, my most cordial greeting, and a special word of confidence and encouragement. Of confidence, because the Church relies a great deal on the value of your suffering, which in the hands of the Lord may become very fruitful for the good of all. Of encouragement, because I assure you of my affection and my prayer, so that you will be able to carry your cross joyfully with the help of God's grace, abundant and comforting, which I invoke for you all.

"Sweet Guest of the Soul"

The following is an excerpt from the Holy Father's address at the general audience on May 21, 1980.

Greeting affectionately all you sick people present here, I wish to remind you of the feast of Pentecost, which we are preparing to celebrate with deep faith and profound joy.

Following the teaching of the Apostle of the Gentiles, we know that the whole creation has been groaning and suffering up to today, and we too, when we are involved in miseries and sorrows of every kind, groan and weep; but the Lord strengthens us and exhorts us to hope always. Know, beloved in Christ, that, in Baptism and Confirmation, the Holy Spirit has been poured into your hearts. Therefore, may He continue to illuminate your minds, in order that you may understand your vocation and the values of your sanctified suffering; may He continue to give you courage and fortitude, so that you may overcome every painful trial with dignity and merit; may He continue, finally, to be always for you the

"Perfect Counselor
Sweet guest of the soul
very sweet relief" (from the Liturgy).

I bless you all, together with those who assist you lovingly.

Power and Mercy of God

The following is an excerpt from an address by the Holy Father at the general audience on May 28, 1980.

A special embrace for you, dear sick brothers! You represent, through your very condition, human weakness, and at the same time the power and mercy of God.

I am close to you with my affection and even more with prayer; but in my turn I commend the needs of the whole Church to your prayers, which are so powerful with God, who "chose what is weak in the world to shame the strong" (1 Cor. 1:27).

May my comforting apostolic blessing help you for this.

You Have God's Approval

The following is an excerpt from the general audience in St. Peter's Square on June 4, 1980.

To you, sick people, my cordial invitation to Christian joy, made mature and deep by the experience of suffering, I wish to recall to you in this connection the comforting words of Saint Peter's first letter: "If when you do right and suffer for it you take it patiently, you have God's approval" (1 Pt. 2:20). The confident and joyful offering of your suffering propitiates the Father's mercy, continues the Son's redeeming work, cooperates in the diffusion of the Holy Spirit in human hearts. In this way you build up the Church and contribute to the good of so many brothers. May my prayer assist you and my affectionate blessing.

Sustained by Faith and Love

The following is an excerpt from the Holy Father's address at the general audience of June 18, 1980.

To you, sick people, present at this meeting, and to all those suffering in body or in soul I would like to recall, with deep affection, how great and moving was the predilection of Jesus for the suffering. May you succeed in bearing your crosses courageously, together with the suffering Jesus, sustained by your faith and your love of Christ. May my blessing comfort you, which I impart to you, to your relatives and to your friends.

"Treasures that Fructify"

The following is an excerpt from the general audience in St. Peter's Square on June 25, 1980.

A very special thought then for the sick and for the suffering who, as at every audience, occupy a privileged place close to the Pope. Beloved sick, I thank you for your precious presence and for the hardship you have had to face to come to this meeting. I am grateful to you particularly for the prayers and hidden sacrifices you offer to the Lord for the Church and the Pope. May the Lord reward you for this. On my part, I exhort you never to lose heart, not even at the most difficult moments that illness imposes on you, and to be always aware that your sufferings are so many treasures that fructify for the good of the society in which we live and to obtain eternal life. May my special blessing comfort you.

With Intensity of Affection

On July 7, 1980, John Paul II met a group of people suffering from leprosy, who had gathered in the courtyard of the archbishop's residence in Salvador da Bahia, Brazil. The Holy Father addressed them as follows.

Beloved sons and daughters,

1. Your presence arouses in my heart a special feeling, something of that emotion and affection that our Lord Jesus Christ felt, during the ministry of His public life, for the sick people who flocked from all sides to hear His Word of salvation and to be cured of their infirmities.

Among so many episodes of cures narrated by the four Evangelists, you will certainly remember the one that St. Luke describes: the sick man who fell on his face and besought Him: "Lord, if You will, You can make me clean." Jesus stretched out His hand, touched him, and said: "I do will it; be clean!" And all the signs of the disease disappeared (cf. Lk. 5:12-13).

The humble Vicar of Christ is among you today with the same intensity of affection with which the Divine Master welcomed and blessed the crowds, and especially the persons afflicted with the same disease that afflicts you.

2. Many people comment that the external purification of the body was the symbol of an interior change: the rebirth of a purity, a confidence, a courage that comes from above. The Pope would like his contact with you to produce these priceless interior sentiments. He exhorts you not to let yourselves be disheartened by fear nor by lack of confidence, not to yield to the temptation of isolation. To unite confidence in the progress of medicine with an attitude of constant and confident prayer.

PAIN IS NEVER FRUITLESS

3. In the name of that same Jesus, whom I represent before you today, I exhort you also to use well and turn to advantage the suffering that you bear imprinted on your bodies and in your spirits. Always remember that pain is never fruitless, never useless. In fact, at the very moment it wounds your existence, limiting it in its human performance, if it is raised to a supernatural dimension, it can exalt and redeem this existence for a superior destiny, which goes beyond the threshold of the personal situation to reach the whole of society, in such need of those who are able to suffer and offer themselves for its redemption.

If you apply to your suffering these great intentions, which go beyond the purely human level, you will collaborate with Christ in the plan of salvation, and you will be capable of spreading around you marvelous examples of moral strength, which only those who suffer with this faith in their soul can communicate to others.

4. I have great confidence in your concern, in your help, and in your prayer, not only for the felicitous outcome of this apostolic journey in Brazil, but also for all the solicitude I bear in my heart as Pastor of the universal Church.

With these thoughts, greeting you warmly and expressing my deep appreciation for those who take care of you and assist you, I entrust you to the motherly protection of the Blessed Virgin, to whom I know that you are very devoted, and I willingly grant you the apostolic blessing.

The Cross of Suffering Is a Source of Grace and Salvation

On July 8, 1980, the Holy Father paid a visit to the Marituba leper colony, in Belem, Brazil. The Pope delivered the following address.

Dear sons,

1. Since I announced my journey to Brazil and during the preparation of this journey, I received from various leper colonies of this country a large number of letters inviting me to visit them. God knows how much I would have liked

to have done so. Coming here to Marituba, meeting you and greeting you with fatherly affection, it is as if I were visiting at this moment all the leper colonies of Brazil. May my word reach them to tell them how much I esteem them, how much I think of them and pray for them.

Blessed be God, therefore, for granting us the grace of this meeting. It is, indeed, a grace for me to be able, like the Lord Jesus whose minister and representative I am, to go to meet the poor and the sick, for whom He had a real preference. I cannot, it is true, cure bodily ills as He did, but He in His kindness will give me that ability to relieve souls and hearts in some way. In this sense I wish this meeting to be a grace for you also. It is in the name of Jesus that we are gathered here: may He be in our midst as He promised (cf. Mt. 18:20).

2. When persons meet for the first time and want to make friends, they usually introduce themselves. Is it necessary to do so? You already know my name and possess some facts about my person. But since I intend to make friends with you, I will introduce myself: I come to you as a missionary sent by the Father and by Jesus to continue to proclaim the kingdom of God which begins in this world but is realized only in eternity, in order to consolidate the faith of my brothers, to create a deep communion among all sons of the same Church. I come as minister and unworthy Vicar of Christ to watch over His Church; as the humble Successor of the Apostle Peter, the Bishop of Rome and Pastor of the universal Church.

In a solemn moment, the Lord Jesus had declared to Simon Peter, despite the fact that, like every human creature he was weak and sinful, that He would build the Church on him, as on a firm rock (cf. Mt. 16:18). He also promised him the keys of the kingdom with the guarantee that whatever he bound or loosened on earth would be bound or loosened in heaven (cf. Mt. 16:19). When Jesus was about to return to the Father, it was again to Peter that He said: "Feed my lambs, feed my sheep" (cf. Jn. 21:15ff.). I come as Peter's Successor: the heir to the mysterious and indescribable spiritual authority which had been conferred on him, but also to the tremendous responsibility entrusted to him. Like Peter, I accepted to be the universal Pastor of the Church, eager to know, love, and serve all the members of the flock entrusted to me. I am here to know you. I must say that my affection for one and all is great. I am sure that I can help you, at least in some way.

FEEL DEEPLY INVOLVED IN THE COMMUNITY

3. And you, who are you? For me you are first and foremost human persons, rich in the immense dignity which the state of person gives you, rich, each one, in the personal, unique and unrepeatable character with which God made you. You are persons redeemed by the blood of Him whom I like to call, as I did in my first letter written to the whole Church and to the world, the "Redeemer of man." You are sons of God, known and loved by Him. You are now, and henceforth

you will always be, my friends, very dear friends. As to friends, I would like to leave you a message on the occasion of this meeting with divine Providence enables me to have with you.

4. My first word cannot but be one of comfort and hope. I know very well that, under the weight of illness, we are all exposed to the temptation of losing heart. One often wonders sadly: Why have I fallen ill? What wrong have I done to deserve it? A look at Jesus Christ in His earthly life and a look of faith, in the light of Jesus Christ, at our own situation change our way of thinking. Christ, the innocent Son of God, knew suffering in His own flesh. The passion, the cross, death on the cross, were terrible ordeals: as the prophet Isaiah had announced, He was disfigured, no longer having a human appearance (cf. Is. 53:2). He did not veil or conceal His suffering; in fact, when it was most atrocious, He asked the Father to remove the cup from Him (cf. Mt. 26:39). But the depths of His heart were revealed by the words: "Not my will, but yours, be done" (Lk. 22:42). The Gospel and the whole of the New Testament tell us that, accepted and lived in this way, the cross becomes redemptive.

Your life is no different. Illness is truly a cross, sometimes a heavy cross, an ordeal that God permits in a person's life, within the unfathomable mystery of a plan that escapes our ability to understand. But it must not be regarded as a blind fatality. Nor is it necessarily and in itself a punishment. It is not something that destroys without leaving anything positive. On the contrary, even when it weighs on the body, the cross of illness borne in union with that of Christ becomes a source of salvation, of life, or of resurrection for the sick person himself and for others, for the whole of mankind. Like the Apostle Paul, you too can affirm that you complete in your bodies what is lacking in Christ's afflictions, for the sake of the Church (cf. Col. 1:24).

I am sure that, seen in this light, illness, even if it is painfully and humanly mortifying, brings with it seeds of hope and new comfort.

5. My second word is a request, but even more an invitation and an incentive: do not isolate yourselves because of your sickness. All those who with dedication, love and competence look after you, even perhaps dedicating all their talent, time, and energies to you, insist on saying that nothing is better than feeling deeply involved in the community of other brothers and not isolated from it. We say in a loud voice to these brothers, with the strength of all our conviction: make an effort to get to know your brother lepers, be close to them, welcome them, cooperate with them, accept and bring forth their cooperation. But to you, too, we must say: do not refuse for any reason to take your place in the environment that surrounds you and that opens up to you. Feel that you are members, to the highest possible extent, of the human community, which is becoming more and more aware that it needs you, as it needs each of its members.

You can offer this community, on the human level, the contribution of the gifts you have received from God. The field of this possible cooperation is, within natural limits, quite wide and varied. On the supernatural level, which is that of grace, I wished to remind you a moment ago that, in union with the mystery of Christ's cross, the cross of your suffering too becomes a source of grace, life, and salvation. It would be a great pity to waste, for any reason, this source of God's grace. May your suffering serve to help many people, and especially the Church. Being in Amazonia, where missionary work is intense and fruitful, and whose fruits you too receive, I venture to ask you: make your condition as sick people a missionary act of immense significance, changing it into a source from which missionaries can draw spiritual energies for their work.

VALUABLE HELP OF YOUR SUFFERINGS

6. My third word is of trust: the Pope, together with the whole Church, esteems you and loves you. He assumes before you and with you the commitment to do everything in his power for you and on your behalf. Even if the Pope has to go off to new tasks, according to the program of this visit and of his exacting mission, he remains with you spiritually: may my dear brother, Mons. Aristide Pirovano, your great friend; may the doctors, the nurses, the assistants who do everything they can for you here, be the Pope's representatives among you, doing everything that he would do and as he would do it if he could always remain here. I, for my part, also rely on you: just as I ask for the help of the prayers of monks and sisters and so many holy persons so that the Holy Spirit may inspire and

give strength to my pontifical ministry, in the same way I ask for the valuable help that can come from the offering of your sufferings and your illness. Let this offering unite with your prayers, or better let it be changed into prayer for me, for my direct collaborators, for all those who entrust to me their afflictions and their sorrows, their needs and their intentions.

But why not begin this prayer at once?

Lord, with the faith You have given us, we acknowledge You are God almighty, our Creator and provident Father, the God of hope in Jesus Christ our Savior, the God of love in the Holy Spirit our Comforter!

Lord, trusting in Your promises which do not pass away, we want to come to You always, and find in You relief in our suffering. However, disciples of Jesus as we are, let not our will, but Yours, be done throughout our whole life!

Lord, grateful for Christ's preference for the lepers who had the good fortune to come into contact with Him, seeing ourselves in them...we also thank You for the favors we receive in everything that helps us, gives us relief, and consoles us. We thank You for the medicine and for the doctors, for the care and for the nurses, for the circumstances of life, for those who console us and who are consoled by us, for those who understand us and accept us, and for others.

Lord, grant us patience, serenity and courage; grant that we may live a joyful charity, for love of You, toward those who are suffering more than we and toward those who, though not suffering, have not grasped the meaning of life.

Lord, we want that our lives be useful, we want to serve, to praise, give thanks, atone and implore with Christ, for those who worship You and for those who do not worship You in the world, and for the Church, scattered all over the earth.

Lord, through the infinite merits of Christ on the cross, a "suffering servant" and our brother with whom we unite, we pray to You for our families, friends, and benefactors, for the successful outcome of the Pope's visit, and for Brazil. Amen.

"Christ Really Saves!"

During the general audience in St. Peter's Square on July 16, 1980, John Paul II delivered an address from which the following excerpt is taken.

And now my thought goes to you, dear sick people, on whose limbs a cross heavier than that of others has been placed.

For you I shall follow the example of Jesus, our Master. When He approaches the sick, or works His miracles for them, He always appeals to the fundamental element that determines the relations of men with God: faith. He seeks it, He revives it, He creates it; because without it His omnipotence comes to a halt.

By means of faith, therefore, that certain faith which trusts God, believes in His goodness, adores His plans, Christ really saves us and creates tranquillity in the ever-agitated sea of the spirit.

May God grant you, dear brothers, His benevolence, and, if it is in accordance with His loving plans, also health of limbs.

"Lord, Grant Us Patience..."

The following is an excerpt from the Holy Father's address during the general audience on July 23, 1980, in St. Peter's Square.

All my attention is now for you, sick people of the archdiocese of Malta who, after having made a pious pilgrimage to the Marian shrine of Lourdes, have wished to stop in Rome, to greet the Pope.

To you and to all the other sick who are here today, even at the cost of inconvenience and sacrifice, I say: rest assured that the Pope is close to you in affection and in daily prayer. Be confident: the Lord will not abandon you. In the most difficult moments of trial turn to Him and say, with the same words that I suggested recently in Brazil:

"Lord, grant us patience, serenity and courage; grant us to live in joyful charity, for love of You, with those who are suffering more than ourselves and with those who, though not suffering, have not a clear view of the meaning of life" (cf. Address at the Leper Colony of Marituba, July 8, 1980).

With this exhortation, I impart to you the strengthening apostolic blessing.

Beatitude of Tears

During the general audience in St. Peter's Square on July 30, 1980, the Holy Father delivered an address from which the following excerpt was taken.

And to you, beloved sick brethren, who, in suffering and infirmity, are united in a special way with Jesus, I address a greeting full of affection and cordiality and, interpreting also the sentiments of those who are present at this audience, I hope that you will be able to live in fullness the "beatitude of tears" (cf. Mt. 5:4), proclaimed by Christ for His most faithful followers. The way of the cross is, on the human plane, very hard, but it leads to light, peace, and endless joy.

I willingly impart to you all a special apostolic blessing, commending myself and the whole Church to your prayers, made precious by suffering.

Heritage and Splendor

The following is an excerpt from the address given by Pope John Paul II during the general audience on August 6, 1980.

To you, beloved sick, I address my loving and grateful greeting.

Two years ago, in the evening of Sunday, August 6, Pope Paul VI left this earth for heaven. For the Angelus of that day he had written: "The transfiguration of the Lord casts a dazzling light on our daily life.... That body which is transfigured before the astonished eyes of the Apostles is the body of Christ, our brother, but it is also our body called to glory; that light which floods Him is and will be also our share of heritage and splendor" (*Insegnamenti di Paolo VI,* 1978, p. 588).

May these last words of the great Pontiff be a consolation and encouragement to you in your sufferings, together with my blessing.

"Our Home Is Heaven..."

On August 13, 1980, continuing the catechetical cycle begun some weeks before, the Holy Father delivered an address of which the following is an excerpt.

I have great pleasure in turning my affectionate and grateful thought also to those dear ones among us who are ill.

As Paul the Apostle says: "We know that our home is in heaven where we also await our Lord Jesus Christ the Savior, who will change our vile body that it may be fashioned like his glorious body" (Phil. 3:20-21). Holy Mary has already reached her heavenly home, and after exile on earth she gained entrance immediately to glory. So, let your sufferings, your anxieties, your hopes be directed towards her, in the certainty that her help in joining her after this exile on earth will not fail.

With this wish I bless you all from my heart.

Jesus Gives Meaning and Energy to Our Every Pain and Suffering

On September 14, 1980, the Pope met the patients of Annunziata, Italy, the city hospital that faces the Square of Siena's Cathedral. The Holy Father addressed the sick and the hospital staff.

Dearest brothers and sisters,

It is with joy and anxiety that I address my cordial greetings to you on the occasion of this visit to the dear city of Siena. I certainly could not forget you, who among the limbs of the Body of Christ, which is the Church, are most worthy of attention and concern.

I have come among you to bring the assurance of my heartfelt sharing of your sufferings. Know that the Pope is near you with special affection, and above all prays for you that the Lord may alleviate your pain and even more grant that you face it with inner strength and evangelical spirit.

When we Christians go through the experience of pain, we must be careful to give it the right meaning. It is not a punishment, but an occasion for purification of our sins; in particular, its end is the good of men, our brothers, as it was for Jesus, who gave His life as a ransom for all (cf. Mk. 10:45). Therefore, through faith, join your tribulations to those suffered by Him. We should carry our crosses in His footsteps, otherwise they become too heavy. But with Jesus Christ before us, we walk more quickly, since He gives meaning and strength to every pain of ours.

Accept also my most heartfelt wishes for a rapid and total recovery, in accordance with God's will. And may the special conciliatory apostolic blessing that from my heart I extend to all of you, to your dear ones, and to all those who attentively take care of you, be a pledge of my affection.

Raise Your Eyes to Heaven

During the weekly general audience in St. Peter's Square, on October 8, 1980, the Holy Father gave an address from which the following excerpt was taken.

Dear sick people, if you can raise your eyes to heaven and take the inheritance of tears from God, you, too, will have a part in the song of heavenly life, which never passes away.

Consoling Mystery of Redemption

On October 22, 1980, Pope John Paul delivered a message to the faithful gathered in St. Peter's Square for the weekly general audience. The following is an excerpt from that talk.

A very special greeting goes to the sick people gathered here. Beloved in Christ, I thank you for your presence, always so significant. It says that you are fully part of the Church, and, in fact, are members in quite a special way. For what the suffering have in common with Christ reminds everyone that, precisely through His sufferings, He redeemed us from the alienation of sin and reestablished our communion with God. To you, therefore, goes my wish, as well as the assurance of my prayer, in order that you may be able to penetrate more and more the consoling mystery of redemption which does not elude, but on the contrary necessarily includes human suffering. And let my fatherly blessing accompany you.

"By Means of Our Cross..."

The following is an excerpt from an address delivered by the Holy Father to the faithful gathered in Saint Peter's Square on October 29, 1980.

Beloved sick! Last Sunday, as you know, the Church officially declared Blessed, with Don Orione, also Bartolo Longo, the well-known founder of the Sanctuary of Our Lady of the Rosary at Pompeii. Reading his biography, we are impressed by the many moral and spiritual sufferings he had to undergo and which accompanied the creation of the sanctuary—the continual goal, also today, of immense multitudes, and a place of conversion and sanctification. This is a great lesson for you, sick people, and for everyone. By means of our cross, God carries out the work of salvation. May my apostolic blessing accompany you, bringing consolation.

Courage and Fortitude

During the weekly audience on November 12, 1980, the Holy Father delivered an address from which the following excerpt was taken.

To you, dear sick people, my no less cordial greeting. Jesus Christ came into the world, died and rose again for everyone; to you, tried by suffering, Jesus addresses His gifts of courage and fortitude with greater attention and care; you are more dear to Him.

May your faith be great and your prayer confident! May you be comforted by my blessing, which is for you and for all those who are with you, in your affection and in your necessities.

In Your Old Age Accompany Christ to the Cross

On November 19, 1980, in the cathedral in Munich, Germany, the Holy Father met with representatives of a notable part of the German populace, the elderly. The Pope offered them the following message.

My dear brothers and sisters who are advanced in age!

It fills me with special joy that during my visit to Germany I am allowed to meet with you in a special hour of prayer. I come as to familiar friends; for I know that in my service I am supported in a special way by your concern, prayer, and sacrifice. So I greet you here in the Cathedral of Our Lady in Munich with heartfelt gratitude. I thank you especially for the profound words of welcome and for your prayer by which you accompanied me during these days. Together with you I greet all the people of your age group in your country, especially those who through radio and television are united with us in this moment. *Grüss Gott* to all of you who longer than I have "endured the work and heat of the day" (Mt. 20:12), who longer than I have exerted yourselves to meet the Lord and to serve Him in all fidelity, in the great things and in the small ones, in joy and in suffering!

1. The Pope bows with devotion before old age, and he invites all people to do the same with him. Old age is the crown of the steps of life. It gathers in the harvest, the harvest from what you have learned and experienced, the harvest from what you have done and achieved, the harvest from what you have suffered and undergone. As in the finale of a great symphony, all the great themes of life combine to a mighty harmony. And this harmony bestows wisdom—the wisdom which young King Solomon is praying for (cf. 1 Kgs. 3:9-11) and which means more to him than power and riches, more than beauty and health (cf. Wis. 7:7, 8, 10)—the wisdom about which we read in the rules of life of the Old Testament: "How attractive is wisdom in the aged, and understanding and counsel in honorable men! Rich experience is the crown of the aged, and their boast is the fear of the Lord" (Sir. 25:5f.).

To today's older generation, that is to you, my dear brothers and sisters, this crown of wisdom is due in a very special way: some of you had to see and to endure immense pain in *two* world wars; many of you have thereby lost your relatives, your health, your profession, your house and your home country; you have come to know the abyss of the human heart, but also its ability for heroic willingness to help, and for loyalty to the Faith, as well as its power to dare a new beginning.

Wisdom confers distance, but not a distance which stands aloof from the world; it allows us to be above things, *without despising them;*

it allows us to see the world with the eyes—and with the heart!—of God. It allows us with God to say "yes" even to our limitations, even to our past—with its disappointments, omissions, and sins. For "we know that in everything God works for good with those who love him" (Rom. 8:28). From the conciliative power of this wisdom spring up kindness, patience, understanding, and—that precious ornament of age—the sense of humor.

You yourselves know best, my dear sisters and brothers, that this precious harvest of life which the Creator has apportioned to you is not an uncontested possession. It requires vigilance, carefulness, self-control, and sometimes even a resolute battle. Otherwise it is endangered, easily to be eaten away or to be corroded by idleness, by moods, by superficiality, by arrogance, or even by bitterness. Do not lose heart; with the grace of our Lord start over and over again, and use the sources of power which He offers you: in the Sacraments of the Bread and of forgiveness; in the Word which comes to you in sermons and in reading and in spiritual conversation! In this place I am sure that I am allowed also in your name most cordially to thank the priests who reserve a decisive place in their work and in their hearts for the pastoral work among the aged. In this way they at the same time render the best service to their whole community; for thereby they win for it, in a sense, a legion of faithful intercessors.

Next to the priests who serve you with their pastoral work I should like to address myself to the priests of your age group. My dear confreres!

The Church thanks you for your lifelong work in the vineyard of the Lord. To the younger priests Jesus says in the Gospel of John: "Others have labored, and you have entered into their labor" (4:38). Most venerable priests, keep on bringing the needs of the Church before God through your priestly service of prayer—"*ad Deum, qui laetificat iuventutem vestram*" (Ps. 43:4)!

A TREASURE TO THE CHURCH

2. Brothers and sisters of the older generation, you are a treasure for the Church, you are a blessing for the world! How often you have to relieve the young parents, how well you know how to introduce the youngsters to the history of your family and of your home country, to the tales of your people and to the world of faith! The young adults with their problems often find an easier way to you than to their parents' generation. To your sons and daughters you are the most precious support in their hours of difficulty. With your advice and your engagement you cooperate in many committees, associations and initiatives of ecclesiastical and public life.

You are a necessary complement in a world which shows enthusiasm for the vitality of youth and for the power of the so-called "best years," in a world where what can be counted counts so much. You remind it that it continues building upon the diligence of those who were young and strong *earlier*, and that one day it, too, will place its work in younger hands. In you it becomes apparent that the meaning of life cannot consist in earning and spending money, that in all our external activities there has to mature something internal, and something eternal in all the temporal—according to the words of St. Paul: "Though our outer nature is wasting away, our inner nature is being renewed every day" (2 Cor. 4:16).

Indeed, old age deserves our devotion, a devotion which also shines forth from Holy Scripture when it places before our eyes Abraham and Sara, when it calls Simeon and Anna to the Holy Family in the temple, when it calls the priests "elders" (cf. Acts 14:23; 15:2; 1 Tm. 4:14; 5:17, 19; Ti. 1:5; 1 Pt. 5:1), when it sums up the worship of the whole of creation in the adoration of the twenty-four elders, and when finally God calls Himself: "the Ancient of Days" (Dn. 7:9, 22).

ACCEPT THE BURDEN OF OLD AGE

3. Is it possible to intone a higher song in honor of the dignity of old age? But, my dear elder listeners, I am sure you would be disappointed if the Pope would not also mention another aspect of becoming old; if he would have brought you only—maybe unexpected—the honors, but would have failed to bring you consolation. Just as to the beautiful season in which we are not only belongs the harvest and the solemn splendor of color, but also the branches being stripped of their leaves, the leaves falling and decaying; not only the soft and full light, but also the wet and dreary fog—in the same way old age is not only the strong final accord or the conciliative sum of life, but also the time of fading, a time where the world becomes strange and life

can turn into a burden, and the body into pain. And so I add to my call, "Be aware of your dignity," the other one, "Accept your burden."

For most people the burden of old age means in the first place a certain frailty of the body: the senses are no longer as acute, the limbs no longer as pliable as they used to be, the organs become more sensitive (cf. Sir. 12:3f.). The things one may experience in younger years in days of sickness, often become one's daily—and nightly!—companions in old age. One is forced to give up many activities which used to be familiar and dear.

Also the memory may refuse its service: new facts are no longer received easily, and old ones fade away. And so the world ceases to be familiar: the world of one's own family with the living and working conditions of the adults utterly changed, with the interests and forms of expression of young people so completely different, with the new learning goals and methods of the children. The home country becomes strange with its growing cities, the increasing density of population, and the landscape many times remodeled. The world of politics and economics turns strange; the world of social and medical care becomes anonymous and unintelligible. And even that domain where we should feel at home most of all—the Church in her life and doctrine—has become strange to many of you through her effort to meet the demands of the time and the expectations and needs of the younger generation.

By this world which is hard to understand, you feel misunderstood and often enough rejected. Your opinion, your cooperation, your presence is not asked for—that is how you feel and how, unfortunately, sometimes it actually is.

A REDEEMING SUFFERING

4. What can the Pope say to this? How shall I console you? I do not want to make it too easy. I do not want to belittle the anxieties of old age, your weaknesses and illnesses, your helplessness and loneliness. But I would like to see them in a conciliatory light—in the light of our Savior "who for us did sweat blood, who for us was scourged at the pillar, who for us was crowned with thorns." In the trials of old age He is the companion of your pain, and you are His companions on His way of the cross. There is no tear you have to shed alone, and none you shed in vain (cf. Ps. 5:9). By His suffering He has redeemed suffering, and through your suffering you cooperate in His salvation (cf. Col. 1:24). Accept your suffering as His embrace and turn it into a blessing by accepting it from the hand of the Father who in His inscrutable yet unquestionable wisdom and love is using just this to bring about your perfection. It is in the furnace that metal turns into gold (cf. 1 Pt. 1:7); it is in the press that the grape becomes wine.

In this spirit—which God alone can give us—it becomes also easier to be understanding with those who through negligence, carelessness, heedlessness, contribute to cause our need, and it becomes possible for us to forgive also those who knowingly and even intentionally make us suffer without, however, completely conceiving how much pain they cause us. "Father, forgive them, for they do not know what they are doing!" (Lk. 23:34) Also with regard to us has this word been spoken which alone brings salvation.

MODEL IN ST. ELIZABETH

5. In this Spirit—whom we want to implore together and for each other in this hour—we are also going to be awake and grateful for all loving thoughts, words, and deeds which we receive each day, which we so easily get used to and which therefore we easily take for granted and which we overlook. We are celebrating today the feast of St. Elizabeth, a saint your nation has given to the whole world as a symbol of self-sacrificing charity. She is the sublime example and great patroness for all who serve their fellow creatures in need—be it through their profession or on a volunteer basis; be it in the circle of their friends and relatives—and who meet Christ in them, whether they know it or not. That, my dear elder people, is the reward which you give to those for whom you dislike being a burden. You are the occasion for them to meet the Lord, the opportunity to outgrow themselves, and by your turning to them you let them share in the already mentioned fruits of life which God allowed to mature in you! Therefore do not bury your requests in a timid, disappointed or reproachful heart, but express them in all naturalness—being convinced of your own dignity and of the good in the hearts of the others. And be

happy over each opportunity to practice that royal word of "thank you" which rises from all altars and which is going to fill our eternal beatitude.

And so I am sure that I will be allowed together with you to thank all those people who work for the well-being of the older generation, for their well-being in body and mind, in order to help them find a fulfilled life and a permanent home in society, all those who work in the many ecclesiastical, civil and public organizations, associations, and initiatives, on a communal or on a higher level, in legislature and administration, or just on a private basis. I commend especially the fact that working *for* the elder people is becoming more and more working *with* the elder people.

SOMEONE STILL POORER

6. With this I turn again to you, my elder brothers and sisters, and to the consolation you expect from me. There is a saying: "When you are lonely, go and visit somebody who is still lonelier than you!" This wisdom I would like to recommend to you. Open your mind for those companions on your road who, in whatever respect, are still in a poorer condition than you, whom you can help in one way or the other—through a conversation, through giving a hand, some favor, or at least your expressed sympathy! I promise to you in the name of Jesus: in this you are going to find strength and consolation (cf. Acts 20:35).

In this way you simultaneously practice in small matters what we all are as a whole. We are one body in many members: those who bring help and those who receive help; those who are more healthy and those who are more sick; those who are younger and those who are older; those who have stood the test of life, those who are still standing it, and those who just are growing into it; those who are young and those who once were young; those who are old and those who are going to be old tomorrow. We all together represent the fullness of the Body of Christ, and we all together mature into this fullness—"into the perfect man, fully mature with the fullness of Christ" (Eph. 4:13).

CONSCIOUS OF DEATH

7. The last consolation we are seeking together, my dear fellow pilgrims "in this vale of tears" *(Salve Regina)*, is the consolation in the face of death. Since our birth we have been going to meet it, but in our old age we become more conscious of its approaching from year to year—if only we do not forcefully suppress it from our thoughts and feelings. The Creator has arranged it so that in old age accepting and standing the test of death is being prepared, made easier and learned in an almost natural manner. Because becoming old, as we have seen, means a slow taking leave of the unbroken fullness of life, of the unimpeded contact with the world.

The great school of living and dying, then, brings us to many an open grave; it makes us stand at many a deathbed before it will be us around whom other people will be standing in prayer—so may God grant it. An old person has experienced such lessons of life in a greater number than young ones do, and he is seeing them with increasing frequency. That is his great advantage on the way to that great threshold which we often in a biased way conceive of as being an abyss and night.

The view across the threshold is dark from our side; but those who have gone before us God will allow in His love to accompany our lives and to surround us with care more often than we possibly think. It has been the conviction of deep and living faith which gave to a church in this city the name of *All Souls Church.* And the two German churches in Rome are called: *Santa Maria in Campo Santo* and *Santa Maria dell'Anima.* The more the fellow beings of our visible world reach the limits of their ability to help, the more we should see the messengers of the love of God in those who already have passed the test of death and who are now waiting for us over there: the saints, especially our personal patrons, and our deceased relatives and friends whom we hope are at home in God's mercy.

Many of you, my dear sisters and brothers, have lost the visible presence of your partner. To you I direct my pastoral admonition. Allow God ever more to be the partner of your lives; then you will also be united to the one whom He gave you as a companion once upon a time and who himself now has found in God his center.

Without familiarity with God there is in the last end no consolation in death. For that is exactly what God intends with death, that at least in this one sublime hour of our life we allow ourselves to fall into His love without any other security than just this love of His. How could we show Him our faith, our hope, our love in a more lucid manner!

One last consideration in this context. I am sure it echoes the conviction of many a heart. Death itself is a consolation! Life on this earth, even if it were no "vale of tears," could not offer a home to us forever. It would turn more and more into a prison, an "exile" *(Salve Regina)*. "For all that passes is just a parable!" (Goethe, Faust II, final chorus) And so the words of St. Augustine, which never lose their color, come to our lips: "You have created us for Yourself, Lord; and our heart is restless until it finds its rest in You!" *(Confessiones I,* 1, 1)

And so there are not those who are destined to die and those who stand in the so-called life. What is awaiting all of us is a birth, a transformation whose pains we fear with Jesus on the Mount of Olives, but whose radiant exit we already carry within ourselves since at our Baptism we were submerged into the death and victory of Jesus (cf. Rom. 6:3-6; Col. 2:12).

Together with all of you, together with you here in our Lady's cathedral, with you before radio and television, with all those whom I was allowed to meet in these blessed days, with all the citizens and guests of this beautiful country, with all those who believe, and for all those who are seeking, with the children and young people, with the adults and the old people, I would like in this hour of farewell to turn our meditation into prayer!

"Upon you I have leaned from my birth; forsake me not when my strength is spent!" (Ps. 71:6, 9)

"Come to our aid with your mercy and keep us safe from temptation and sin, so that we may be full of confidence as we await the coming of our Savior Jesus Christ!" (Order of the Mass)

And here in our Lady's cathedral I would like to combine our prayer, which always is spoken in the Spirit of Jesus and only through Jesus arrives at the Father, with the prayer of the one who, being the first to have been saved, is our Mother and our Sister (Paul VI at the conclusion of the third session of the Council *Insegnamenti* II, pp. 675-664):

"Holy Mary, Mother of God, pray for us sinners now and at the hour of our death! Amen."

Amen—Praised be Jesus Christ!

Your Suffering Is Prayer

At Balvano, a little town in the province of Potenza, Italy, almost completely destroyed by the earthquake on November 23, 1980, the Pope met the parish priest and the few survivors and spoke to them as follows.

Praised be Jesus Christ! Beloved brothers and sisters, I have not come here out of curiosity, but as your brother and your pastor; I come for a reason of human solidarity; I come for a reason of compassion, of charity. You are surrounded by this compassion on the part of all—all your fellow countrymen, all Christians. I want my stop in your little town of Balvano to be a sign of this human solidarity and this Christian charity. What I say for your town, I say also for the neighboring ones, such as the one whose name I cannot repeat at this moment: but there are certainly so many others, whose names I could not repeat at once. Rest assured that I come for everyone. Someone said to me: "But these people cannot pray anymore." This is my answer: "You, beloved, pray with your suffering." And I hope, I am convinced, that you pray more than so many others who pray, because you bring to the Lord this great suffering of yours, these victims of yours, especially the young people, the children, who died in the church. I see how your parish priest is suffering: I met him a short time ago. That is all I can say to you at this moment. I have come to tell you that I am close to you. Christ said to the Apostle Peter: "Strengthen your brothers." I cannot strengthen you with my human powers, with my human capabilities, but I can strengthen you in the sense that together we can find the power of Jesus, in Jesus, in our faith and our hope, in His charity which is greater than all sufferings, greater even than death, because even with death this charity of His opens up to us the perspective of life. The perspective of life opened to us by Jesus suffering on the cross and by the risen Christ is the one that must open before you all, who have suffered the death of so many dear ones, of your children, or perhaps your old people, who have passed through such a painful cross. I would not like to speak anymore, beloved, to multiply words. I bring you above all the living testimony of my presence, my compassion, my heart, and of a special memory that I wish to keep of this town, of all the neighboring ones, of all the suffering, of all this area, of the environment, hit so hard, of your country, sorely tried in these regions, of all of you as Christians and brothers and sisters. I offer you, at the end of these words, my blessing: the blessing of your Pope, the Successor of Peter, and the blessing of your brother in suffering.

In the Hope of Resurrection!

In the course of the visit Pope John Paul II paid on November 25, 1980, to the areas of Campania and Basilicata, Italy, devastated by the earthquake, the Holy Father brought his comfort to many people hospitalized in Potenza. The Pope spoke to them as follows.

I wish to express my thanks for the words with which I have been introduced on this occasion. I felt a duty, an impulse of the heart, of conscience, to come here, to be, at least partially, closer to you suffering people, to you who have suffered and to you who are suffering.

This interior necessity is certainly caused by compassion, not by a sensation. By human and Christian compassion. You victims of the earthquake, injured, stricken, homeless—and with you, your dead—are certainly surrounded by the human and Christian compassion of all your fellow countrymen, of the whole of Italy, and you are surrounded especially by the compassion of the Church. And I come, beloved brothers and sisters, to show you the meaning of this closeness, to tell you we are close to you, in order to give you a sign of that hope which one man must be for the other. For one who is suffering, a healthy man; for one who is wounded, a doctor, and someone to assist him, a nurse; for a Christian, a priest. So one man for another man. And when so many men are suffering, so many men, many men, are needed, to be close to those who are suffering.

I would say, continuing the words of your pastor, your bishop: I cannot bring you anything more, anything more than this presence; but with this presence, with this visit, a relatively short and partial one, everything is said. And I beg you to receive with this partial visit a total attitude, a total response to your suffering.

I said that when men suffer, when a man suffers, another man is needed, close to the one who is suffering. Near him. For in this way, what your bishop has stressed comes true. The presence of Christ in both comes true—in the suffering man and in the man who is close to him, who assists him. And, with Christ's presence, the world, even though stigmatized with the cross, bears in it the hope of resurrection. A world stigmatized by death—there are so many dead in this region, it is already being written that the number is 3,000—bears in it the hope of life. A world stigmatized by ruins bears in it the hope of new life, of reconstruction, because life and charity cannot be indifferent in the face of destruction. They try to reconstruct, they try to redo, to give the human environment a human character, a human dimension once more. These are the feelings, the expressions that well up from my heart. And as you see, they come with difficulty, because emotion is greater than the possibility of speaking and formulating ideas well.

I want to speak to you only with my presence, and with this service of presence. Sometimes there remains to us principally or only this form of carrying out our service, our human and Christian and priestly ministry. There remains only this: presence. But, there is also my blessing. I would like to bless all those present, especially all the suffering, the hospitalized, but also all the professors, doctors, men and women nurses, and all those who assist the sick and the suffering, and all those who are still working in the places hit by the earthquake, in search of persons who are still under the ruins.

I want to bless you all from the bottom of my heart with the words and with the grace that the blessing of Peter's Successor brings.

"Favorites of the Gospel"

On December 3, 1980, the Holy Father gave an address to the thousands gathered in the Paul VI Hall, of which the following is an excerpt.

To all of you who are suffering because of illness I address an affectionate thought and say to you: the Pope is particularly close to each of you, and remembers you in prayer. If the Lord does not abandon anyone, far less could He forget you, dear sick people, who are the favorites of the Gospel: "Blessed are those who mourn, for they shall be comforted" (Mt. 5:4). But you, in your turn, offer your sufferings, which are a precious treasure before God, for the Church, for the conversion of sinners and for the salvation of all souls. With my apostolic blessing.

In Imitation of Mary

During the general audience on December 10, 1980, in the Paul VI Hall, the Holy Father gave the following address, of which the following is an excerpt.

Dear sick people, I call upon you to address a thought of fervent devotion to Mary, the joy of our hearts, the consoler of all those who suffer. Even if we are tried by pain, we cannot but rejoice in our God, who has clothed us with the garments of salvation and with a robe of righteousness (cf. Is. 61:10), in order to be capable of changing our suffering into a loving offer, in imitation of our Lady, the Co-redeemer. May Mary nourish in you sentiments of serenity and hope, and may she strengthen also the blessing, which I impart to you from the bottom of my heart.

Solidarity and Scientific Research To Overcome Suffering and Isolation

On December 13, 1980, the Holy Father received in audience the participants in the twenty-fourth work session of the International Federation of Associations Against Leprosy (ILEP), which includes associations from twenty-four industrialized nations who work in close collaboration with eighty countries in which leprosy is endemic. John Paul II delivered the following message.

Dear friends,

1. I am very pleased to have this meeting with you, the delegates of the ILEP. Through you I greet those people who, with generous sensitivity, have taken upon themselves a noble cause to which they daily devote their energies of mind and heart. Your Federation of Anti-Leprosy Associations, which includes the Associations in twenty-four industrialized countries and which works in close collaboration with some eighty countries where leprosy is endemic, performs the praiseworthy task of facing the problem of this disease in a unified manner; thanks to the proper coordination of initiatives and efforts, it is careful to avoid waste and delay.

On this occasion I am happy to be able to tell you how much I appreciate the lofty aims that inspire your work. I am likewise glad to offer you a word of encouragement to continue as you have begun. I myself have had some personal experience of the work being done to combat this disease: I was able to visit leprosaria during my pastoral visits to both Africa and Brazil. The amount of progress that still remains to be made is considerable, if we are to rely upon the statistics which tell us that at the present time no more than twenty percent of the people affected by Hansen's disease receive medical treatment. There still remain in the world millions of sufferers who are left to fend for themselves and who are exposed to the consequences of an illness that generally presents little resistance to adequate therapy. This is a fact that cannot fail to be on the conscience of anyone with Christian, or merely human, feelings.

2. You carry out your activities according to a worldwide strategy that seeks to take into account all the needs of the people concerned, both on the level of health and on the economic and social levels. For this purpose, in harmony with the programs drawn up by the Alma Ata Conference of the World Health Organization, you have set yourselves the task of making your contribution on the level of "basic medicine," which counts upon the responsible participation of the communities to which your assistance is directed, in the work of prevention and cure.

You also strive to go beyond any form of therapy that would involve the isolation of the sufferers. By means of the provision of proper mobile services, it is in fact possible to offer patients the necessary treatment, enabling them to remain with their families and to continue working.

It is easy to see the advantages of this mode of procedure: besides sparing the sufferers the always traumatic experience of isolation, it helps to overcome the age-old prejudices and unjustified fears that still prevail in certain sections of society. The superstitions surrounding leprosy must be dispelled, in order to render ever more effective the various forms of combating it that are already providentially being used in the world.

3. The associations belonging to your federation, as also the other organizations working in this field, are also directing their efforts to the sphere of scientific research. The directions being taken by these studies are numerous, and some are proving particularly promising: I am thinking of the research being done on the Hansen's disease bacillus, research which is seeking to determine its exact biochemical composition, to identify its characteristics more accurately, to measure the efficacy of new drugs, and to produce as soon as possible an effective anti-leprosy vaccine.

The financing of this research, as also the production of already known drugs, which are very effective and rapid but also very costly, calls for considerable economic resources. The funds which you can count upon are not sufficient to meet these requirements. You are therefore rightly engaging in an ever wider effort to alert society, with the aim of bringing home to every individual the plight of so many brothers and sisters who, simply because they are sick, find themselves condemned to a segregated and brutalized existence.

I am happy to encourage you in this humanitarian campaign. And I cannot fail to express the hope that the generosity of private individuals will be matched ever more by the efforts of international organizations and governments, so as to bring about a full and lasting victory in this far from hopeless battle.

4. This hope, which cannot fail to receive the support of every person of good will, certainly evokes a special echo in the hearts of those who recognize in Christ the Son of God, who through love became the brother of every human being. How can Christians fail to feel the challenge of that hard saying: "As you did it not to one of the least of these, you did it not to me" (Mt. 25:45)?

The Church is preparing to relive, in the mystery of Christmas, the wondrous event of the entry into human history of the Word made flesh. It was an event marked by poverty and rejection, by the hostility of some and the indifference of the majority. From the crib, in which He lay surrounded by simple shepherds—a category regarded as "impure" by the society of that time—the Son of Man asks every believer how much he or she is doing to combat not only the bacillus of Hansen's disease but also the bacillus of so many other forms of leprosy, originating and developing in the contagious bacillus of selfishness.

May the contemplation of this prodigy of God's love serve to foster in the hearts of the faithful renewed resolutions of fraternal solidarity; may it bring to you all the consolation of experiencing once more the truth of that "saying" preserved for us by the Apostle Paul: "It is more blessed to give than to receive" (Acts 20:35). With this good wish I willingly invoke upon you, your fellow workers and all who support your work with their generous contributions, the abundant blessing of Almighty God.

Ecclesial Communion Draws Nourishment from Sacrifices of Those Who Suffer

On December 21, 1980, the Holy Father went on a pastoral visit to the Hospital of St. James in the Augusta section of Rome. In the course of his visit the Pope delivered the following address.

Beloved brothers and sisters!

1. After the visit I paid in December of last year to the chief Hospital of the Holy Spirit in Sassia and to the Pious Institute of the same name, I deeply desired to come to this nosological center, dedicated and, as it were, consecrated to nursing and caring for the sick. If we consider, in fact, its antiquity and its history—a history of nearly seven centuries—it has claims to due consideration that are not inferior or secondary, and it takes its place worthily because of the qualified activity that is still carried out here in the very vast and multiform framework of the socio-medical organization and of the hospital

structures of the city. Today it is an important part of the "Local Health Unit, Rome One."

But I have come—as you well understand—not so much to point out the external elements, important though they are, that distinguish Saint James, as to meet, in keeping with the nature of my mission as Bishop of Rome, the people who are here. I wish, therefore, to greet the political and administrative authorities, beginning with the President of the Regional Council of Latium and the President of the Management Committee of the aforementioned Health Unit, whom I thank for his kind welcoming address.

As a shepherd who wishes to be and must be close to the sheep of his flock, I am thinking also of all those who are working here as medical operators, and those who are suffering here from the pains of illness. I am thinking of you physicians, assistants and nurses, and above all of you, beloved sick brothers and sisters: I now wish to greet all of you, one by one, in the Lord's name. I see among you Mons. Fiorenzo Angelini, who has been actively engaged in the hospital apostolate for so many years, and with him are the zealous chaplains, the nursing sisters, the pastoral council of the hospital and the well-deserving volunteers for assistance to the sick; therefore, I willingly extend my cordial greeting to them too.

LOCATION OF HOSPITAL— A STRATEGIC CHOICE

2. Right from the beginning, St. James' Hospital had its center here, and the choice was

certainly not a casual one. As in the case of the Holy Spirit Institute, the well-deserving founders and promoters were concerned that it should rise in an area close to Via Cassia and Via Flaminia, so often traveled by pilgrims on their journey of faith and piety towards the city consecrated by the martyrdom of Saints Peter and Paul. It could be said that it was a "strategic choice," intended to offer to those who arrived in Rome from the north after such fatigues and also, in some cases, after the dangers of a long journey, welcome and assistance, and when there were sick people, also aid and hospitalization.

I will not dwell upon the extraordinary and constant solicitude that the Pontiffs, my Predecessors, had for this hospital throughout the centuries, entrusting it to special confraternities for its management, awarding it the title of Archhospital and intending it for those who were affected with diseases once considered "incurable," or better, "not curable" (cf. Bull *Salvatoris nostri*, of Leo III, dated July 19, 1515; *Bullarium Romanum*, t. III, p. III, 418-420; cf. *ibid.*, 421-423).

I consider another fact far more important, since it indicates an outstanding spiritual level: in the age of the Italian Renaissance St. James was an active school of charity for some great figures of saints. St. Cajetan of Thiene made it his habitual dwelling for many years in order to be near his sick brothers and sisters. St. Philip Neri frequented it from his youth as a place for exercising piety, and he was among the first to foresee the opportunity of ensuring convalescents a period of rest in a suitable place before resuming work. St. Felix of Cantalice, so popular in sixteenth century Rome, who often came to help his Capuchin confreres who were active here in his time. But the name of St. Camillus de Lellis is more closely connected than others with Saint James. He spent here, at various times, almost a decade of his life, which was not a long one, as a patient, attendant, nurse and bursar. After conversion from the dissipation of his youth, in the ancient church of St. James attached to the hospital, he celebrated his first Mass, and it can be said that it was precisely from the deeply felt and concrete experience matured here, that he drew such wise lines of pastoral action, which he subsequently fixed in the rule of his congregation of "Servants of the Sick." Even today his spirit hovers within these venerable walls, and—we can add—he still is active here thanks to the presence and dedication of "his" religious.

3. But today's meeting would run the risk of remaining abstract and impersonal, if there were not on my part a distinct and direct word for the persons who, with their presence and with their work, enliven the reality of the hospital as real promoters. I address in the first place you esteemed doctors and professors who, with your collaborators, have the primary responsibility of treating the sick, in need as they are of human understanding and brotherly love, even before effective and appropriate therapies. I know very well the difficulties of various kinds which are characteristic of your profession: in addition to sacrifices that can easily be recognized—which

are called the duty of presence, promptness of intervention, "standing by" in emergency cases—there is the necessity to keep up-to-date in the medico-scientific field, which in our days, due to the incessant rhythm of research and experimentation, is in a state of permanent development.

SERVICE TO THE SICK

All this can be summed up in one word, which only apparently may seem usual and common: it is the word "service," to be understood as a struggle against disease and a commitment to the sick. Yours is actually a service of life, or even better, of the living man, that is, that man who—as a great father of the ancient Church says—precisely because he is living, is, in the concrete, the glory of God: *Gloria Dei homo vivens* (St. Irenaeus, *Adversus haereses* IV, 20, 7). From this depth of perspective there emerges all the grandeur and nobility of the medical profession, which is at the same time an art and a science, because alongside a serious doctrinal preparation it requires keen psychological intuition. If life is a gift from God—a great gift from God—it must constitute for you the terminal and inescapable reference point, to which you must continually look in all the individual services and phases in which the exercise of such a delicate art is carried out. Your service is addressed precisely to living man, from the first moment in which this ever new and amazing mystery of life buds, thus deriving immediately a character of sacredness. Here is the first principle, the absolute principle, which concerns professional ethics and does not admit of exceptions and violations: it must be, therefore—and I hope it will always be—a point of honor.

Yes, honor! *Honora medicum*, the ancients said, and I wish to repeat it now, as just recognition of your merits before human society and also in confirmation of the esteem with which the Church has always followed and encouraged your work!

4. And now I wish to address you, dear Camillian religious and Reverend Sisters of Mercy, who dedicate your assiduous pastoral care to the sick. When I recalled just now the four figures of saints whose memory is here in blessing and in perennial example, I was thinking especially of you, because it is from them that your beneficial daily work must draw inspiration. Like the doctors, you too are assigned to a service, obviously a different one, which concerns specifically the religious and pastoral sphere. What are the qualities of such a service? How can we call them? Discretion, gentleness, thoughtfulness, sensitivity, capacity for starting, resuming or developing—according to the different psychological conditions or circumstances of the person —a dialogue of faith? Yes, certainly: but it is better to use the more exact word, which is offered by Christian vocabulary. The Servants of the Sick and the Sisters of Mercy have charity as their uniform and endeavor to act as Jesus, the Divine Master, as that "Son of man (who) came not to be served but to serve, and to give his life as a ransom for many" (Mt. 20:28; Mk. 10:45).

Act in such a way, brothers and sisters, that, in the luminous wake of the saints who imitated Christ the Lord here, the most genuine and solicitous charity may be the sovereign moderator of all that you do for the benefit of the sick.

REQUEST FOR PRAYERS

5. Finally, I address my word to you, sick brothers and sisters, you who have been able to come here, and also you who, because of your conditions of health, have remained in your sections, rooms, and wards. This word descends from that same flame of evangelical charity which I recently recommended as a guiding virtue to your chaplains and sisters.

When on October 17, 1978, immediately after my unexpected elevation to the pontificate, I went to the polyclinic "Agostino Gemelli," I did not obey just an impulse of the heart to visit some friend there, at Monte Mario. I wished to give then—and I can confirm it two years later—a precise indication about the way in which I conceived and conceive the awesome ministry of Peter's Successor. On that occasion I told the sick that I relied on them a great deal, a very great deal: through their prayers and, above all, through the offering of their suffering, a special power could be drawn for me, a power that was and is necessary for me to carry out in a less unworthy way my heavy duties within the Church of Christ. This same idea of an ecclesial communion, encouraged and made more valuable by the mysterious, yet very real, contribution of the sacrifices of the suffering, I now express again before you. I repeat, therefore, that I rely a great deal on you, and thank you for this help of yours, while on my part I commend each of you to the Lord who, as He is the master of life, so He is the Father of mercies and consolations (cf. Sir. 23:1; Wis. 11:26; 2 Cor. 1:3).

GIFTS OF PEACE, JOY, BROTHERHOOD

6. Drawing to a conclusion, I cannot forget that my coming coincides with the eve of the Christmas festivities and is, therefore, tuned to a typical and inspiring atmosphere of intimacy and human warmth. Christmas does not only bring back to us a past memory, but actualizes in history the coming, among us men, of Jesus as our Savior. Here at St. James' I have met you sick people who, brothers and sisters of Christ, are also my brothers and sisters, and precisely because you are in this place, you resemble Him even more. Particularly united and close to you, I anticipate with you, this very evening, the celebration of the birth of the Lord. May there always be in you and in all brothers and sisters, beginning with your relatives and with those who lovingly assist you, the heavenly gifts of peace and joy, brotherhood and love. This is my wish, which I willingly confirm with the apostolic blessing!

Year of the Handicapped

The following is an excerpt of the address given by the Holy Father on the World Day of Peace, January 1, 1981.

As is known, 1981 has been proclaimed by the U.N. "The International Year of Handicapped Persons." There are millions of persons suffering from congenital infirmities, chronic illnesses, or affected by various forms of mental deficiency or physical disabilities, who, in the course of this year, will appeal more intensely to our human and Christian conscience. According to recent statistics, their number amounts to over 400 million. They, too, are our brothers and sisters. Their human dignity and their inalienable rights must receive full and effective recognition throughout the whole span of their existence.

Last November, during the meeting of a working group, the Pontifical Academy of Sciences, in its constant work in service of mankind through scientific research, made a thorough study of a particular category of handicapped persons, the mentally handicapped. Mental debility, which strikes about three percent of the world population, must be taken into special consideration, because it is the most serious obstacle to man's fulfillment. The report of the above-mentioned working group stressed the possibility of preventive treatment of the causes of mental debility by means of suitable therapies. So science and medicine offer a message of hope and at the same time of commitment for all of mankind. If only a minimum part of the budget for the arms race were assigned for this purpose, important successes could be achieved and the fate of many suffering persons alleviated.

At the beginning of this year I wish to entrust all handicapped persons to Mary's motherly protection. During Easter of 1971, four thousand mentally handicapped persons, divided into little groups accompanied by relatives and educators, were pilgrims in Lourdes and lived days of peace and serenity together with all the other pilgrims. I hope and trust that, under Mary's motherly gaze, experiences of human and Christian solidarity will be multiplied, in a renewed brotherhood that will unite the weak and the strong in the common path of the divine vocation of the human person.

THOSE WHO SUFFER

On the threshold of this new year, thinking of the most serious needs of mankind, I would like to call attention next to that part of the human family that is in dire need because of the food situation. Hunger and malnutrition are today, in fact, a tragic problem of survival for millions of human beings, especially children, in vast areas of our globe. My thought goes particularly to some vast regions of Africa struck by drought, such as Sahel, and of Asia, damaged by natural calamities or which have to cope with a considerable influx of refugees.

According to a report of the Food and Agriculture Organization, at least twenty-six African countries have had recent harvests inferior to those of the past. In some parts of that continent hunger persists and periodic famines take place, which take their toll of victims. According to the calculations of experts, moreover, world grain stock will drop for the third year running, if the present trend continues. I hope from the bottom of my heart that all those in charge, all organizations and all men of good will, will make their contribution for the implementation of measures that will permit more effective aid for brothers and sisters in want and, at the same time, that a more effective system of food supply will be created. The words of Christ, "I was hungry and you gave me food," are an impelling and particularly relevant reminder of our responsibilities.

St. Paul's words in today's liturgy are penetrating ones. The life of the large human family all over the world must be changed under the sign of the universal brotherhood of men. In fact, we are sons: God has sent the Spirit of His Son into our hearts, crying: Abba, Father. So no one is a slave any longer, but a son!

Gift of His Strength

On January 7, 1981, the Holy Father resumed his weekly audiences which had been suspended because of the Christmas holidays. The following is an excerpt of his message.

To you, the sick, most dear to me, on whom the divine Redeemer has bestowed the mysterious gift of suffering, goes my affectionate greeting and that of the whole People of God. May

Jesus, who became a frail and weak Child, give you also the gift of His strength, which is that of donation, dedication, and concealment. I entrust the whole Church to your meritorious suffering, in order that she may always have the constancy and the strength to be an open witness to the death and the resurrection of Jesus Christ. My apostolic blessing is intended to be a source of comfort for you and for your dear ones.

"...With Christian Fruit"

The following is an excerpt of the Pope's message in the Paul VI Hall, January 28, 1981.

I address a very special greeting to the dear sick people gathered here, among whom there is a group of children and a woman from the Social and Health Center of Torre Spaccata, together with the volunteer nurses of the Italian Red Cross who assist them.

My beloved children, I tell you at once all the great affection I have for you, which your presence today increases even more. I would like to be able to relieve your sufferings, and I assure you that you have a very special place in my prayer for this intention. I earnestly commend you to the Lord, that He may give you all the strength necessary to live your condition with Christian fruit. Trust Him fully. And know that I am close to you with the concern of a father, who blesses you wholeheartedly.

"A Precious Seed..."

In the general audience of February 4, 1981, the Pope gave an address of which the following is an excerpt.

A word of greeting, comfort and encouragement also to the dear sick, because of the place of special predilection they occupy in my heart. You have come here, overcoming the difficulties of the journey, but bringing also the riches of your courage in facing up to the discomforts of everyday life.

Your suffering can be compared to the seed which, in the season of winter, develops slowly, while waiting to blossom in spring. Such is the suffering of a sick person: a precious seed which will receive unhoped-for rewards from the Lord, the symbol of that cross which regenerated the world and caused the buds of Christian communities to bloom everywhere.

The Pope remembers you in prayer and blesses you willingly.

Abandonment to God's Will

In the general audience of February 11, 1981, the Holy Father gave an address, of which the following is an excerpt.

Addressing my affectionate thought to you, beloved sick, there comes into my mind the image of Lourdes, "Mary's Citadel," where the Immaculate Mother of Jesus appeared as a vision of light and hope to recall men to heavenly realities, and to comfort and heal the sick in spirit and in body. The story of Lourdes is a poem of Mary's motherly love, always vigilant and concerned about her children, and it also sums up the history of so much human suffering, which has become prayer, offering, confident abandonment to God's will, drawing from it comfort, serenity, meaning and value for one's own suffering. May the Blessed Virgin, from the Grotto of Massabielle, give to you too, as to so many sick people, today and always, a smile, an encouragement, a grace, that will relieve you and comfort you on your way of suffering. With these wishes I bless you.

You Are Not Alone, Dear Sick People

Following the tradition of a Sunday Angelus message, the Holy Father recited the Marian prayer. His brief address of February 22, 1981, in Baguio City, Philippines, was dedicated principally to the sick.

During this visit I have been able to meet a number of sick people in these isles of the Philippines; I have been supported by their smiles and by their prayers. Before leaving, however, I wish to tell all of you who are sick and are suffering how close I am to you in prayer. I wish to reach out to all of you in every home, in every hospital, in every corner of these islands, wherever you are, to assure you of my encouragement, but most of all to prepare you once more for the eternal love of the Sacred Heart of Jesus. There are so many of you who could not come to me, but I pray that now my message can reach each one of you. Remember that Jesus, even in His moments of suffering, was comforted by the presence of His Father. He told us that His Father was with Him: I am not alone; He consoles me. He is with me, He has never left me alone.

My beloved brothers and sisters, it is the same for you: you are not alone, you can never be alone; Jesus and His Father are with you. But even if you should feel alone, you will never be without this element of sacrifice that Jesus is using to bring His dimension into the lives of many people. You sick people of the Philippines, may the love of Jesus Christ sustain you in hope and in the achievement of the great contribution that you can make to mankind by uniting your sufferings to those of Jesus. May the Blessed Virgin Mary help you with her maternal love and be for each of you a consolation in your affliction and the cause of your joy.

"The Suffering, in the Likeness of Christ, Share in the Redemption"

On March 8, 1981, the Holy Father delivered an address to the faithful gathered in St. Peter's Square for the recitation of the Angelus. An excerpt follows.

1. *Christum Dominum pro nobis tentatum et passum, venite adoremus.*

The liturgy of Lent calls us day by day to the worship of Christ, of Him who willed to be subject to temptation and who accepted suffering, becoming for our redemption "sin for our sake" (cf. 2 Cor. 5:21).

We must find this Christ in the inscrutable mysteries of His life and in His death and, at the same time, in our neighbor. In every neighbor, without exception, but particularly in those in whom, in the same way, the temptation and suffering of our Redeemer is repeated and fulfilled.

2. Allow me, therefore, already from the first Sunday of Lent, to call attention to that large number of our brothers and sisters who are defined by the common name of "disabled" persons. The statistics say that there are over 400 million of these persons in the world, that is, about a tenth of humanity. We must hail with gratitude the initiative of the United Nations Organization which wishes the current year to be dedicated precisely to these brothers and sisters of ours, whose lives are spent under the weight of a congenital disability or one suffered as the result of an accident. The UN's initiative is marked by a deep sense of sensitivity and human brotherhood.

The Christ of our Lent, the Christ tried and crucified, is at the very center of this brotherhood. He invites us in a special way to meet Him in each of our suffering brothers and sisters. The love we show them, the service we carry out for them, are proof of love for Him Himself and a service rendered to Him (cf. Mt. 25:40).

3. Lent demands conversion of each of us; therefore—as the liturgy of this season teaches us, from the first days—this conversion is ef-

fected and realized precisely by what we do for our brothers and sisters, in particular for those who suffer and are handicapped in any way. They have a special right to our respect, our esteem and our love.

"In fact, we discover in God the dignity of the human person, of every human person. The degree of physical or mental health does not add or take away anything from the dignity of the person; suffering, in fact, can give him special rights over us."

4. *Christum Dominum pro nobis tentatum et passum, venite adoremus!*

We unite in spirit with one and all of those who are suffering, affected by an incurable disability. Among everything we can offer them, there is also our faith, and namely the conviction of their particular likeness to the suffering Christ.

And if inner suffering—greater than the disability itself—may sometimes become for them a reason for considering life absurd and empty, then, from the depth of this faith, we wish to tell them and bear witness with conviction that they, through their suffering, take part in a special way in the mystery of the redemption of the world, which Christ accomplished through the cross.

"Always Be Close to Those Who Bear the Cross of Their Disabilities"

On March 14, 1981, the Holy Father received in audience the four hundred delegates at the congress of the National Association of Crippled and Disabled Persons of Work, and delivered the following address.

Beloved brothers and sisters!

At the end of the spiritual exercises which provided me a special interval for a more intense lifting of the spirit to God the Father in prayer and reflection, I am happy to meet you, worthy representatives of the National Association of Crippled and Disabled Persons of Work.

1. I extend to all the members of this society my cordial greeting and an affectionate welcome, expressing my deep thanks for the noble expressions with which your president introduced this friendly meeting. I cannot fail to express to you, in the first place, my deep feeling of satisfaction and esteem for the appreciated work that you carry out in protection and defense of the "moral and material interests"—as the second article of your statutes rightly say—of all those tried in body and in spirit by the consequences of tragic accidents at work in the various fields of human activities.

My appreciation goes particularly to the praiseworthy contribution you make to solve the problems of your members and for their reintegration into social life, saving them from loneliness and moral discouragement, starting them along the way to a necessary human relationship. The network of specific assistance in this connection, spread all over the national territory, is a clear testimony of your valuable and effective activity.

2. All that cannot but meet with the encouragement of the Church, which is constantly undertaking initiatives in order that every person—but in particular those most exposed to exclusion because of their precarious health conditions—may be guaranteed his inalienable dignity, human, social and spiritual. In this connection, precisely in these days, the Holy See has expressed in a document "deep gratitude to all communities and associations, to all men and women religious, to all lay volunteers who devote themselves to the service of disabled persons, bearing witness to the perennial vitality of that love which knows no barriers." At the same time it urged that every individual, suffering on account of any handicap, should be helped to "become aware of his dignity and his values and to realize that something is expected of him and tnat he, too, can and must contribute to the progress and good of the family and its community" (cf. *L'Osservatore Romano,* English edition, March 23, 1981). The Catholic Church sees in you, therefore, valuable allies in her mission of human advancement and evangelization, and is ready to offer her support and her organizations in order to attain these ideals. You can imagine from this how fervently she hopes that your welfare activity will spread more and more and be

increasingly effective for all those who have paid a personal price—and still bear its mark in their suffering flesh—to provide their own family with bread and contribute to the prosperity of society.

3. Ladies and gentlemen, please accept a last word of exhortation and good wishes: always hold your activity in very high esteem, which will continually urge you to reach new goals in this vast and delicate field in which you are called to carry out your work of elevation and brotherly consolation. Never be satisfied with what you have done and never let the difficulties tire you. Read in the eyes and in the hearts of those who bear the cross of their mutilations and disability, having to sustain hard struggles, often hidden from men, but known to God and strengthened by faith in Him. Be close to those you assist and let them feel the warmth of your true friendship, which like a fragrant balm can comfort so many hearts and soothe so many sufferings. In addition to the sense of justice, which is at the basis of every human relationship, have also and above all loving understanding, because as I wrote in the recent Encyclical *Dives in misericordia*, "society can become ever more human only if we introduce into the many-sided setting of interpersonal and social relationships, not merely justice, but also that 'merciful love' which constitutes the messianic message of the Gospel" (no. 14). Only in this way will you be able to perceive, beyond the man or woman in need of help, the face of the suffering Christ, who in this holy season of Lent is presented to us by the liturgy as the Servant who is without beauty or

splendor (cf. Is. 53:3). May the Lord be your support and your reward, strengthening your efforts with reflections of eternal merit.

This is the wish that I very favorably form for you all and for all the members of your association, and that I accompany with the conciliatory apostolic blessing.

With Love and Generosity

The following is an excerpt from the text of the Holy Father's address given during the weekly general audience on March 14, 1981.

To you, beloved sick people, who are suffering and who desired nevertheless to take part in this audience, I want to express my affectionate greeting in a very special way. I thank you for your significant presence, and above all for the example you set by accepting to carry out God's will with love and generosity. In this season of Lent through which we are passing and at the approach of Holy Week, I am happy to say also to you what I affirmed at Anchorage, in Alaska: "Let us never let ourselves be thrown into confusion by the suffering that may enter our life, but let us rather try to transform it in the light of the cross of our Savior Jesus Christ. May our trust always be placed in the Holy Spirit to discover, in every situation, a new opportunity to extend Christ's redeeming love" (February 26, 1981, Homily at Delaney Park).

May my comforting apostolic blessing help you.

Unite Your Cross With His

The following is an excerpt from the address given by the Holy Father to those attending the general audience of March 18, 1981.

What words shall I address now to you, dear sick people? In the first place receive my most cordial greeting: I bid you welcome here. If Jesus was full of such feeling for all the suffering, as the Gospel informs us, His Vicar, the Pope, cannot but be so close to you and your tribulations.

I would now like to add: we are in the holy season of Lent, which takes place entirely, for everyone, under the predominant sign of the Lord's cross. The Lord willed His cross; He could have kept it far away, but He willed it, and He willed it out of love, love for us, to give us the gifts of grace and salvation, courage and serenity. Beloved in Christ, in your hours of sadness, looking to Jesus, unite your cross lovingly with His! Your soul will be greatly consoled, and your life will accumulate countless merits; and you too, though in concealment, can be, with your faith and your love, missionaries, apostles, priests. Nourish these generous intentions, which are very pleasing to our Divine Redeemer. May my blessing come upon you with my fatherly affection.

"Take Your Place With Faith in the Mystery of the Cross"

The meeting of the Holy Father with the sick and the sisters of the diocese took place in Terni Cathedral, March 19, 1981. John Paul II delivered the following address.

Beloved brothers and sisters!

1. With very intense sentiment I greet all of you who bear in your spirit and your body the weight and the painful sign of the cross of Christ and who, with your human suffering, are united with, and integrated into, the Paschal Mystery in a quite special way.

I am here with you, beloved in Christ, to tell you that a spiritual union binds me to every person who suffers; whether he is immobilized and confined to a bed or to a chair; or whether, because of his own suffering and disability, he considers himself now useless; or whether he sometimes feels, like Christ at Gethsemane, "greatly distressed and troubled" (cf. Mk. 14:33).

I sincerely feel that my words are insufficient and inadequate to express to you my sincere sympathy, my human compassion. Yet, together, you and I firmly believe, in the light of the Word of God, that there exists a dimension beyond the control of the senses or of mere human reason, in which your suffering and that of all men and women takes on deep significance and is transformed from weakness to strength, from poverty to riches, when it is illuminated by the cross of

Jesus. "God chose what is weak in the world to shame the strong...so that no human being might boast in the presence of God" (1 Cor. 1:27, 29). Just as for the salvation of men the heavenly Father chose the cross, a sign of ignominy and weakness, so He chose your infirmity, in order that this cross, placed on your shoulders and cut into your flesh, may become—together with that of Jesus—an instrument and sign of salvation for you, who bear it in faith and in Christian hope, and for all other men in need of salvation. Then you will really be able to say with St. Paul: "I will all the more gladly boast of my weaknesses, that the power of Christ may rest upon me. For the sake of Christ, then, I am content with weaknesses...; for when I am weak, then I am strong" (2 Cor. 12:10).

2. Therefore I ask you, brothers and sisters present here, and all those who are suffering in Terni in hospital wards or in their homes, to take your place with faith in the mystery of Christ's cross, offering your human sorrow to Him, so that He, uniting it with His, may offer it to the Father in a pure oblation. With suffering and with prayer you can do immense good in favor of the Church and of mankind.

The saints, true Christians, illuminated by the grace of the Spirit, realized the meaning and the fruitfulness of their suffering.

In this cathedral there is a tomb on which these simple and touching words can be read: "Giunio Tinarelli, a witness to faith and love in suffering." You know who Giunio Tinarelli was:

a fellow citizen of yours, born in 1912, and so your contemporary. At the age of twelve, to earn his living, he began to work, first at the Alterocca Printing Press and then in the Terni steel works. But when still very young he was stricken with a terrible disease, which immobilized him for eighteen years until his death, which took place in 1956, at the age of forty-four. In that immobility, in that suffering, what faith, what love your Giunio communicated to those who went to visit him, not to comfort or console him, but to receive consolation and comfort from him!

Remembering this exemplary Christian, I ask you to pray and offer your sufferings for humanity, for the Church, and also for me, so that my universal pastoral service may always be carried out according to God's will. And on behalf of mankind, the Church and myself, I say to you: "Thank you!" May the Lord, rich in mercy, give all of you peace and interior joy and reward with His grace also those who, with generous unselfishness, lovingly take care of you: the members of your families, friends, doctors, nurses, priests and sisters.

I take advantage of the presence of the doctors of Terni to thank them for their care of the sick of the province. I do the same for the nurses: I thank everyone on behalf of Christ, who so attentively evaluated all help offered to a suffering person. Once more I say thank you to all you brothers and sisters.

3. I then wish to address my cordial and affectionate greeting to all the sisters of Terni,

gathered in this cathedral for today's meeting, which is intended to be a mutual uplifting of the spirit.

Beloved sisters in Christ! When you heard in your hearts, through inscrutable ways, the call to follow the "vocation," you answered generously with the words of the Blessed Virgin: "Behold, I am the handmaid of the Lord; let it be done to me according to your word" (Lk. 1:38).

Always keep in mind that the "religious vocation" is a singular treasure of the Church and that your presence within the People of God must be for everyone a visible sign of the Gospel. Your apostolate, so varied, so multiform, so productive of good, is a continual sign of the perennial vitality of the Mystical Body of Christ, in which you bring—with your generous dedication and your admirable hidden life—that particular sensitivity of mothers and sisters in the spirit.

I wish to repeat to you here today what I said to sisters in my apostolic pilgrimage to Mexico: "Yours is a vocation which deserves the highest esteem on the part of the Pope and the Church, yesterday as today. For this reason I wish to express to you my joyful confidence in you, and encourage you not to be discouraged along the way that you have undertaken, which is worth continuing with renewed spirit and enthusiasm.... How much you can do today for the Church and for mankind! They are waiting for your generous commitment, the dedication of your free heart, expanding in an unsuspected way its potentialities of love in a world that is losing its capacity for altruism, for self-sacrificing and disinterested love. Remember, in fact, that you are mystical brides of Christ and of Christ crucified" (English weekly edition of *L'Osservatore Romano*, February 12, 1979).

Like the Blessed Virgin you have chosen Jesus, to whom you are bound with the sacred and sweet bonds of poverty, chastity and obedience. Live in serene joy and fulfill these vows with generous dedication, always faithful to the specific charism of your congregations!

On all of you, brothers and sisters, I invoke the abundance of the Lord's gifts and I willingly impart to you the apostolic blessing, a sign of my affectionate favor.

"Special Role of the Handicapped in Advancement of Human Values"

The Second International Games for the Disabled, Roma '81, *were held in Rome from April 2-5, 1981. On April 3, the Holy Father met some 400 participants in the cortile di San Damaso and delivered the following address.*

Dear brothers and sisters,

1. I am happy to have this opportunity to meet you, and I am pleased that the Second International Games for Disabled Persons, *Roma '81*, has brought you together. The games for which

you have come show clearly and effectively that handicapped persons can be and are fully integrated into social life. They show that you live a full life and share in its joys.

Sports for you are not a matter of economic interest. You have not come to set up new absolute records in the various branches of athletics. However, your participation in sports sets up a record that from many points of view is far more important: a record of surpassing yourselves, a record of universal brotherhood through sports and of practicing solidarity with all members of the human family.

2. I therefore congratulate all who were involved in organizing the games. They include the International Stoke Mandeville Games and the International Sports Organization for the Disabled, the Italian National Olympic Committee, the *Federazione Italiana Sport Handicappati*, and the authorities of the region of Lazio and of the province and city of Rome. My congratulations also go to the organizers and participants in the scientific congress being held in conjunction with the games and dealing with medical, juridical and technical problems of the disabled. I congratulate you all for offering assistance to the disabled, for opening up for them possibilities of improving their lives, and for giving them hope.

3. I am glad to note that greater sensitivity is now being shown with regard to the needs of the handicapped. What gives rise to this sensitivity and sustains it is greater awareness of the value and dignity of the human person, which do not

depend on secondary qualities such as strength and physical appearance, but on the fundamental fact that he or she is a person, a human being.

4. With this goes awareness of the duty of solidarity with all members of the human family, who have a right to be integrated into the different forms of the life of society. Accordingly, we must endeavor to put an end to discrimination, not only by one race against another, but also by the strong and healthy against the weak and sick. In a document issued earlier this month, the Holy See has stressed the basic principles concerning the disabled, who are full human subjects, with the corresponding rights, and must be helped, in accordance with the principles of integration, normalization and personalization, to take their place in society in all aspects and at all levels, as far as is compatible with their capabilities.

5. It is important that the greater awareness and sensitivity now existing should be embodied in appropriate legislation and that those who are active in the fields of medicine, psychology, sociology and education should foster the full integration of the handicapped person into society. But it is no less important that there should be a change of heart, a conversion, on the part of every citizen and every group in society, so that they may willingly and fraternally accept the presence of handicapped persons at school, at work and in every activity, including sports.

6. Handicapped persons play an important part in creating a new civilization, the civilization

of love, by removing social barriers and bringing in new values, the values not of force but of humanity.

7. In Jesus Christ there is an important message for all the disabled, and for those who serve the disabled, and for society as a whole in its relations with them. Jesus Christ brought us a message that has emphasized the absolute value of life and of the human person, who comes from God and is called to live in communion with God. The same message can be read in His own life of love for the sick and suffering, and of service to them. The message also comes from the words with which He identified Himself with all those in need and indicated that His disciples should be known for their loving service of the poor and the weak: "As you did it to one of the least of these my brethren, you did it to me" (Mt. 25:40).

I pray that His message will be heard, and that fresh hope will be given to the disabled, and that new love will permeate all society.

Be Always Ministers of Life, Never Instruments of Death

On April 5, 1981, the Holy Father visited the Roman Hospital of St. John Calibita on the Tiber Island, on the occasion of the fourth centenary of the presence of the Fatebenefratelli in Rome. John Paul II delivered the following address.

Beloved brothers and sisters of Fatebenefratelli Hospital!

1. Praise be to God who has made possible this meeting with you, guests of this ancient and

well-deserving hospital of the Tiber Island! I thank the Lord who has enabled me to talk to you, to express to you my sincere affection.

I wish to greet the Prior General of the Hospitaler Order of St. John of God, Brother Pierluigi Marchesi, thanking him for his kind welcome and for the consoling words with which he wished to introduce this meeting.

An equally affectionate greeting goes also to all the members of the board of directors; to the Cardinal Vicar Ugo Poletti; to Bishop Fiorenzo Angelini, in charge of spiritual assistance in the hospitals and clinics of Rome; to the illustrious physicians: head physicians, senior assistants and assistants; to the clerical, paramedical and auxiliary personnel; to the chaplains, sisters, the group of volunteer workers and all those who in various ways carry out here their precious work of human and Christian solidarity in behalf of the dear sick. I greet everyone and I address my encouragement and appreciation to everyone in the name of the Lord Jesus who, during His earthly life, gave special attention to the sick and cured all kinds of diseases (cf. Mk. 1:39; Lk. 4:44; Mt. 9:35). I address these same thoughts also to all the men and women nurses, on whom the smooth operation of the hospital depends to a great extent, because they are the closest collaborators of the doctors and the assistants closest to the patients.

ORIGINS ENVELOPED IN LEGEND

2. Finding myself here, on the occasion of the fourth centenary of the arrival in Rome of the

Religious of the Hospitaler Order, better known by the name of *Fatebenefratelli,* I cannot fail to recall the long period of history that has been unfolded here. Its origins are even enveloped in the aura of legend, according to which the first nucleus of this refuge was a ship that was submerged in the muddy waters of the Tiber. It is certain that already in the time of the Romans this mysterious island was used as a place of treatment. But it was in the sixteenth century, after years of abandonment, that it resumed its medical purpose in the light of Christian love, which is the characteristic of the followers of Christ and which St. John of God succeeded in instilling so well in his spiritual children who have run this hospital with loving and admirable care for centuries.

Their presence in Rome goes back, in fact, to 1581, when a small number of Brothers began to care for the poor at a little hospital in Piazza di Pietra, amid the imposing columns of the ancient temple of Hadrian. The work of assistance, carried out with Christian piety by the first Spanish and Italian religious, soon attracted the esteem, the respect and the veneration of the citizens, so that that first site ended up by being too small to hospitalize and treat all the poor who turned to the charity of the religious. It was then that the hospital was transferred from that place to this more spacious and comfortable site in 1584. In nearly 400 years of activity it has restored health and the joy of life to countless sick of so many generations, who have in these four centuries succeeded one another in this hospital. The approval and thanks of Rome, of the Church and of the Pope therefore goes to the *Fatebenefratelli* for this blessed beneficial work, which is their true claim to glory.

THE NOBLE WORK OF DOCTORS

3. Together with the religious who direct this hospital, my spontaneous and due thought goes to all the physicians who have worked in the past and are working today for the treatment and relief of the patients.

Beloved doctors, I willingly take this opportunity to reaffirm also to you, as I have already done on other occasions, the benevolence, the esteem and the hope that the Church places in you and in your experience in such a noble and generous mission as that of service to suffering brothers and sisters. I am happy, in this connection, to borrow the words that my venerated Predecessor Pius XII addressed to a group of surgeons in 1945: "How elevated, how worthy of every honor is the nature of your profession! The doctor has been designated by God to meet the needs of suffering humanity. He, who created this being, consumed by fever or lacerated, whom you see here in your hands; He who loves him with an eternal love has entrusted to you the ennobling task of restoring him to health. You bring to the sick person's room and to the operating table something of the charity of God, of the love and tenderness of Christ, the great Physician of the soul and the body. This charity is not a superficial sentiment which lacks firmness.... It is, in fact, love which embraces the whole person, a being who is a brother in humanity, and whose sick body is still animated by an immortal soul, whom all the rights of creation and of redemption unite with the will of his Divine Master" *(Discorsi e Radiomessaggi*, VI, p. 304).

DOING ALL FOR LOVE

I wished to quote this stupendous passage of Pius XII's address because it highlights the mission of doctors and the human and Christian solidarity they must show together with their doctrine and with the advances of experimentation. You, too, under the severe scientific investigation which is always necessary for a precise diagnosis, be inspired by humanity and a deep sympathy towards those who have recourse to your help. Be always ministers of life; never, never, instruments of death! Do everything with love, for love of Christ, who will not leave unrewarded all that you do for the humblest of His fellowmen, because He wished to identify Himself with each of them: "*Quamdiu fecistis uni de his fratribus meis minimis, mihi fecistis*" (Mt. 25:40). "As long as you did it for one of these least brothers of mine, you did it for me."

May this ideal motive sustain you in your profession: may it be the secret heartbeat that ennobles your efforts; may it be the sacred commitment that makes you perceive in the suffering, especially in the most abandoned, the painful face of Christ and His grateful expression. Let yourselves be guided by these sentiments in the care of your patients and "the God of love and peace will be with you" (2 Cor. 13:11).

SHARING IN THE MYSTERY OF THE CROSS

4. And what shall I say to you, dear sick people, present at this meeting or in the wards of this hospital? Once more I express to you my greeting and particular affection. And then I will tell you that you are dear to me: not only because of the charity that we all owe to one another, but also because of the particular claim you have to sharing more than others in the mystery of the cross and of redemption; you are dear to me because pain confers on you a dignity that merits preference of affection; you are dear to me because I see in you the treasures of the Church, which is continually enriched with the gift of your sufferings; you are dear to me because you are pilgrims on your way towards heaven, following a difficult and steep path and passing through the narrow door; you are dear to me because the blessedness reserved by Christ for those who suffer, belongs to you. So be blessed!

Is it necessary to remind all of you, sorely tried by suffering, who are listening to me, that your pain unites you more and more with the Lamb of God, who "takes away the sin of the world" through His passion? (Jn. 1:29) And that therefore you, too, associated with Him in suffering, can be co-redeemers of mankind? You know these shining truths. Never tire of offering your sufferings for the Church, that all her children may be consistent with their faith, persevering in prayer and fervent in hope.

I repeat forcefully to you today what I said at Cottolengo in Turin: "With your pain you can strengthen hesitant souls, bring back to the right way those who have strayed, restore serenity and confidence to those in doubt and anguish. Your sufferings, if accepted generously and offered in union with those of Christ Crucified, can make an outstanding contribution in the battle for the victory of good over the forces of evil, which are lying in wait for modern humanity in so many ways" (*Insegnamenti di Giovanni Paolo II*, III, 1, 1980, p. 874).

Accept and live your experiences of pain in this light: never refuse to make a gift of your sacrifices and your hidden sufferings to the Lord and to the Church: you yourselves will be the first to have merit and reward.

MESSAGE OF HOPE

5. Beloved brothers and sisters, at the end of my talk with you on this evening of the fifth Sunday of Lent, I cannot but reecho the announcement of hope, which we listened to in the proclamation of the Gospel of the Mass today. Before working the miracle of the resurrection of Lazarus at Bethany, Jesus makes a solemn proclamation about Himself, which would give to generations and generations of Christians throughout the centuries hope that does not disappoint, in fact, a firm certainty. The Lord says to Martha, the sister of Lazarus: "I am the resurrection and the life; he who believes in me, though

he die, yet shall he live, and whoever lives and believes in me shall never die" (Jn. 11:25-26). As Son of God, Jesus is not only a mediator for His faithful, but also the author or efficient cause of that superior life which conquers death and is given not only on the last day, but every day. The Lord asks Martha, and therefore all of us, for this faith. Let us likewise answer, together with Martha, with a profession of faith in Jesus the Messiah: "Yes, Lord; I believe that you are the Christ, the Son of God, he who is coming into the world" (Jn. 11:27). Let us, too, recognize Christ as our Lord, as He who stands in front of us, as He stood in front of that tomb of Lazarus in Bethany. We, too, have need of resurrection. Is not our whole life a rising again from evil, from disease and from death? But let us not fear, there is a Savior, there is Jesus Christ among us. He stands in front of us and cries to us as He did to Lazarus: "Come out!" (Jn. 11:43) Come out of your physical and moral infirmity, your indifference, your sloth, your selfishness and the disorder in which you live. Come out of your despair and your restlessness, because the time announced by the prophets has come, the time of salvation, in which "I will raise you, O my people.... I will put my Spirit within you, and you shall live" (cf. Ez. 37:12-14).

Let us live our earthly existence with this hope and with this perspective, which gives our life calm, inner serenity, profound peace and confidence, in the common certainty that in us there is not a fragment of life that is not destined to rise again with Christ.

In this spirit, as we approach the holy Easter celebrations, I heartily express to one and all of you fervent wishes for Christian joy and continual resurrection in Christ, our Redeemer.

With my apostolic blessing.

"I Am with You at Lourdes in Prayer and Thought"

During Holy Week, 1981, a pilgrimage of disabled persons, with their parents, relatives and friends, amounting in all to 12,000 people, reached Lourdes, from 23 countries in the world, to celebrate the holy triduum and the festivities of Easter there, in the spirit of Jean Vanier's great association, called Foi et Lumiere, *Faith and Light. The Holy Father sent the following message to all participants in the pilgrimage.*

To the dear disabled persons of "Faith and Light," gathered in Lourdes, to their parents and friends:

In thought and prayer I join your great gathering of pilgrims at the grotto of Lourdes, in these days which are holy for the whole Church and which bring you new peace and light on your way of the cross.

Jesus, having loved His disciples, loved them to the end. This love is for you too, for you in the first place who belong to the "poor," to those who suffer from limitations in their mind and in their body, but who often understand better than others the need for simple, true relationships, faithful friendship, service freely given, unfailing trust. So enter with Jesus into this charity received and given.

With Him you pass darker moments, which bring you close to the evening of agony and to Good Friday: loneliness, the difficulty of communicating, the fear of not receiving from others the understanding and love to which you aspire, restraints of all kinds which are imposed on you by infirmity and your living conditions. Jesus calls you to put all your trust in the Father in heaven, to offer Him lovingly what hurts you, to forgive others if necessary, to wait patiently for the light which cannot fail to come. You stand at the foot of the cross with Mary, the Mother of Jesus. You approach it with St. Bernadette, so simple, so humble, so poor and so serene.

YOUR PLACE IN THE HEART OF THE CHURCH

Finally, you will take part in the great joy of Easter. God has raised Jesus, His beloved Son; He has made Him the Lord and Savior of all, because He is the only Son of God, and He made Him sit at His right hand, forever, in light. He grants you already to be His children; Baptism, Forgiveness, Communion are as many signs which manifest His love and put the life of the glorious Christ in you, connecting you with His Body. He renews your hearts through His Holy Spirit. He promises you that He will transfigure your whole being, body, intelligence and mind, in a face-to-face meeting.

Already you take your place at the heart of the Church, to live this passover, this passing of the Lord, with all your Christian brothers and sisters. With them, sing the marvels of God! Give freely the joy that you receive freely! Those around you bring you a great deal of assistance and affection; think of the irreplaceable help that you, too, can give to them! The Pope, too, the Successor of Peter, who has wished to tell you again of God's special love for you, also relies on your prayer.

I likewise address the parents, educators, those who accompany you on a voluntary basis, and your friends, so numerous in Lourdes. I would have a great many things to tell you. But already the long document that the Holy See published on last March 4 for "all those who devote themselves to the service of disabled persons" in this year which is dedicated to them all over the world, has expressed to you the "living and vigilant solicitude" of the Church. Reading it will strengthen the convictions, which you have already, about the dignity and the unique value of every human life, about the climate of respect and love with which disabled persons must be surrounded, and about the efforts of integration, normalization and personality development from which they must benefit.

FAMILY SURROUNDINGS

Today I would like to express, above all to you who accompany them so closely in their whole life, the understanding, the sympathy and the encouragement of the Church. The fact that you have accepted and assumed responsibility for your child or friend wounded in his intelligence or his mind, has started you along a difficult and demanding way, which brings with it every day its "shadows" and its "lights." You have realized the importance for this disabled person of having family surroundings, or at least, when that is not possible, of an institution or little community which is close to the family model, in which personalized relations and human warmth enable him to satisfy his duly deep need of friendship and security, while developing his human, moral and spiritual qualities as far as possible.

It is to be hoped that many "volunteer educators" will come to your help, that neighbors will integrate these handicapped persons into normal relationships more and more, instead of excluding them, that the whole of society will show increasing solidarity with your dedication by contributing to the supply of adequate means.

But I hope too that Christian Faith will help you to bear your ordeal with courage, serenity and love, because you, for these children, are witnesses and collaborators in God's tenderness. The wound that you bear yourselves is a participation in the passion of Christ, who took innocent suffering upon Himself; it is also a continual call to freely given love, an opening to God's gift, an appeal to hope. You will take care to initiate them yourselves into these realities, to which they are, moreover, mysteriously close, and the Church will support you with a suitable catechesis. You will help them, also, to become those who give and collaborate, as far as they can, towards a more human world.

May the "Faith and Light" communities and the other initiatives in favor of the mentally handicapped, enable you, beyond this great, joyful and consoling gathering in Lourdes, to find further, and bring to other parents, the necessary support in everyday life! May the Holy Spirit give you His power and His peace! May Mary, Our Lady of Lourdes, keep your hearts turned to the Savior, in hope!

Like my Predecessor Paul VI, I implore on all of you, dear handicapped sons and daughters, parents and friends, the blessing of Christ who died and rose again for us.

Good Friday—A Passing Moment

The following is an excerpt from the address given by the Pope during the general audience on April 8, 1981.

Beloved sick, may my particularly affectionate greeting reach you, who are closest to my heart because of the debt of gratitude that I owe you: I am thinking in fact of the great gift of your prayers and sufferings which you offer to the Lord for my ministry.

Your presence at St. Peter's See is particularly significant in these days, since it coincides with the liturgical season that introduces us to the celebrations of the Lord's passion. Do not forget that Good Friday is only a passing moment to arrive at the joy of Easter, which is fullness of life in the crucified and risen Christ.

Entrust yourselves to Him in your daily prayer, entrust yourselves to Mary, the Mother of Sorrows.

And may you always be accompanied also by my remembrance to the Lord, to which I willingly add the comforting blessing.

The Spirit Helps Us in Our Weakness

During Holy Mass celebrated in the Matilda Chapel on April 11, 1981, the Holy Father conferred the Sacrament of Confirmation on eight handicapped youths who were assisted by the Spastics Group of Cologno Monzese. Three others also received First Communion from the Holy Father. The Pope delivered the following homily

Today I am particularly happy to administer to you, dear boys of Cologno Monzese, the Sacrament of Confirmation. I am happy because with this sacrament you will receive, as you well know, a marvelous gift: the Holy Spirit, the Third Person of the Blessed Trinity. He will descend upon you and dwell within you as in the most beautiful and precious temple.

With Baptism you have already become Christians, sons of God, brothers of Jesus, and members of that community of Jesus' disciples which is the Church. But this gift must now be enriched and brought to completion. And this new grace is precisely the Sacrament of Confirmation. Today the Holy Spirit brings to perfection what He began in you on the day of Baptism. With the Sacrament of Confirmation you will therefore be even more perfectly united with Jesus, and you will become adult and responsible members in the Church. If previously you were like children who only received, now you will be young people and adults who must also learn to give, to grow and to carry out something beautiful and great for the Lord and for your brothers and sisters.

But you will say: What can we do, we who are weak?

Listen to what St. Paul told us: "The Spirit helps us in our weakness.... He intercedes for us with sighs too deep for words" (cf. Rom. 8:26-28). The Holy Spirit gives you power and energy. Among the seven gifts that He brings you there is one that is called fortitude. Do you remember what happened on the day of Pentecost? The Holy Spirit, like a rushing wind, invested with His power the Upper Room where the Apostles were gathered. And those men received extraordinary fortitude and without any more fear they began to preach and to bear witness that Jesus is the Savior of the world. And St. Paul, who had also experienced the power of the Holy Spirit, said: "I will all the more gladly boast of my weakness, that the power of Christ may rest upon me" (2 Cor. 12:9). We will pray, therefore, that the Holy Spirit will grant you the power of faith to believe always in the Lord who saves us; the power of hope always to trust fully in His help and in His kindness for us; the power of love to love the Lord more and more and with one's whole heart and, in Him and for Him, to love one's brothers and sisters; the power of patience to be able to accept our condition with courage and offer our sufferings for the good of souls; the power of good example, to be able to bear witness to goodness and hope to others.

As well as this gift of fortitude, the Holy Spirit will bring you the gift of wisdom, which is, as it were, an inner light of the soul which will make you see and enjoy the beauty of the Lord, His truth and His love. You have listened to what Jesus said in today's Gospel: "I thank you, Father, that you have revealed these things to little ones" (cf. Mt. 11:25).

You are little, but the Holy Spirit can teach you so many important things. He will make you understand who God is; He will make you understand and love the Gospel; He will keep far away from you the shadow of lies and the darkness of error and sin; He will give you pure eyes to see all that is beautiful and good in the spiritual world; shining eyes to see everywhere the presence and the Providence of God the Father beside us, eyes illuminated by joy to teach others too the way to truth and brotherly love.

When the Holy Spirit descended on the Apostles on the day of Pentecost, in the Upper Room, there was also Mary, the Mother of Jesus and our spiritual Mother. Today too, Mary is spiritually present beside each one of you as a Mother. May Mary help us to open our hearts and our minds to receive and always preserve this marvelous gift of the Holy Spirit.

A Common Destiny with Christ

The following is an excerpt from the Holy Father's address given during the general audience on April 15, 1981.

I address a word and special affection to you, too, dear sick people whom faith and the Christian sense of life have brought here, close to memories of Peter. To you I indicate, as well as the bread of the Eucharist, the crucified Christ, whose mystery we celebrate on Good Friday.

I said mystery. Calvary is really a mystery, in fact, where the Son of God is sacrificed for the salvation of men.

Dear sick persons, those who suffer like you have a common destiny with Christ, to participate in a way in His redeeming action, as Saint Paul says: "In my flesh I complete what is lacking in Christ's afflictions" (Col. 1:24). An arduous task, which burns the flesh, and sometimes the heart, but which frees the spirit and makes it worthy of God, and participates in the redemption of the world. May God grant it to you, and may He flood your hearts with peace.

Ever New Hope

The following is an excerpt from the Holy Father's address given during the general audience of April 22, 1981.

I wish to address a particularly cordial greeting to you, beloved sick. I am close to you with my prayer and my affection. I would like to call upon you to contemplate the risen Christ, who has overcome suffering, who has, in fact, saved us precisely by means of suffering and has entered the new and everlasting life of resurrection. Draw ever new hope from the paschal Christ; unite your daily sacrifice with His sacrifice for the good of the Church and of the whole of humanity. Your suffering is not useless when it is united with that of Christ. It is like the drop of water which, poured into the wine in the holy Mass, is transformed into the precious Blood of Christ for the salvation of the world.

The Way of the Cross

The following is an excerpt from an address given by the Holy Father on May 6, 1981.

Here I am greeting you, too, my dear sick, who are always so numerous at every Wednesday meeting. I address the children of the "Italian Care for Spastics" Center of Bosa Marina; the boys chosen by the "Italian Center of Researches for the Self-sufficiency of the Handicapped," as well as the group coming from Sweden and all the others present—a symbol, as it were, of all the suffering there is in the world.

I think that your life may sometimes seem to you useless, and your presence a burden; but it is not so. If we carefully consider the way traversed by Jesus in the sacrifice of Calvary, we learn that suffering is not in vain: Jesus did not do vain things! And if He chose the way of the cross to restore to mankind hope in heaven, it means that the way of the cross, your life, the way also of every follower of the Gospel, is the one which more than any other gathers the treasures of God's benevolence and salvation.

And I urge those who look after your persons to keep always in mind the example and heroism of the saints, who served Christ in the sick and the needy and enriched their lives with countless merits, lives spent in the highest virtue of all, love. May our Lady cause the precious sentiments of faith, hope and charity to grow in all. To this wish I very willingly add my blessing.

"I Have Pardoned Him"

Thousands of people crowded St. Peter's Square on May 17, 1981, to hear the Holy Father's Regina Caeli message which had previously been recorded at his bedside in the Gemelli Hospital. The text of the message is as follows.

Beloved brothers and sisters,

I know that during these days and especially in this hour of the *Regina Caeli* you are united with me.

With deep emotion I thank you for your prayers and I bless you all.

I am particularly close to the two persons wounded together with me. I pray for that brother of ours who shot me, and whom I have sincerely pardoned.

United with Christ, Priest and Victim, I offer my sufferings for the Church and for the world.

To you, Mary, I repeat: *Totus tuus ego sum.* (I belong entirely to you.)

Incomparable Efficacy of Suffering for Implementing the Plan of Salvation

On May 24, 1981, thousands of faithful gathered in St. Peter's Square for the customary Marian prayer. Although they knew the Holy Father would not appear at his window, they had come to pray with him and for him. The following is the message they heard, taped earlier at the Gemelli Hospital.

Praised be Jesus Christ!

Today I wish to address myself in a special way to all the sick, expressing to them—I, a sick man like them—a word of comfort and of hope.

When, on the day following my election to the See of Peter, I came on a visit to the Polyclinic Gemelli, I mentioned that I wished "to entrust my papal ministry particularly to the support of those who suffer."

Providence has ordained that I should return to the Polyclinic Gemelli as a patient. I now reaffirm the same conviction as on that previous occasion: suffering, accepted in union with the suffering Christ, has an incomparable efficacy for the implementation of the divine plan of salvation. I repeat, therefore, with St. Paul: "Now I rejoice in my sufferings for your sake, and in my flesh I complete what is lacking in Christ's afflictions for the sake of his body, that is, the Church" (Col. 1:24).

I invite all the sick to join with me in offering their sufferings to Christ for the good of the Church and of humanity. May Mary most holy sustain and strengthen us.

I then extend my cordial greetings to all those united with me in prayer, and to those who have, during these days, manifested their affection for me, and while thanking them for this spiritual closeness, I assure them of my remembrance in the Lord.

Your Sufferings Increase Charity That Animates the Church

The Pope's message to the International Eucharistic Congress was followed by the following short address to the sick, July 27, 1981.

Dear sick, dear handicapped, dear disabled of the Eucharistic Congress,

My affectionate thought and my prayer go to all the members of the congress, near the Lourdes grotto, but to you in a very special way.

Lourdes is the great place where the sick who have come from all over the world are always in the front row, served by their brothers who are in good health, in order to present their trials to the compassion of our Mother, the Virgin Mary, to the mercy of Christ Jesus, and to set off again with the solace that comes from God.

You are at the heart of the congress which is celebrating the Real Presence of Christ under the humble sign of bread—Christ who suffered and offered His passion in order to enter life and to open His kingdom to us.

You never stop being full members of the Church; not only do you communicate like the others in the body of the Lord, but you communicate in your flesh in the passion of Christ. Your sufferings are not lost: they contribute, invisibly, to the growth of charity, which animates the Church. The Sacrament of the Anointing of the Sick unites you with Christ in a special way, for forgiveness of your sins, for the comfort of your soul and your body, and to increase in you the hope of the kingdom of light and life which Christ promises you.

When I met sick people, in Rome or during my journeys, I liked to stop in front of each of them, to listen to them, and bless them, in order to signify to them that each of them was the object of God's tenderness. This is what Jesus used to do.

God has permitted me, at present, to feel suffering and weakness myself, in my own flesh. I feel all the closer to you. I understand your trial all the better. "In my flesh I complete what is lacking in Christ's afflictions for the sake of his body, that is, the church" (Col. 1:24). I invite you to offer with me your trial to the Lord, who carries out great things through the cross; to offer it so that the whole Church may know, through the Eucharist, a renewal of faith and charity; in order that the world may know the benefit of forgiveness, peace and love.

May Our Lady of Lourdes keep you in hope!

I bless all those who support you with their friendship and their care, and who receive spiritual support from you.

And I bless you yourselves with all my affection, in the name of the Father and of the Son and of the Holy Spirit.

Suffering Nourishes the Grace of Redemption

Before leaving the Agostino Gemelli Polyclinic on August 14, 1981, Pope John Paul II addressed the patients and personnel of the Gemelli Hospital with a message broadcast throughout the whole hospital. The following is the text of his talk.

Dear brothers and sisters,

On May 13, after the attempt on my life, I immediately found effective help in this house which bears the name Gemelli Polyclinic.

Today, after three months, most of which I have spent among you—after the successful and final operation undergone on August 5, the feast of Our Lady of Snows—I am able to return home. Having been restored to health clinically, I am going home to recuperate the strength that is indispensable for the complete exercise of my ministry in St. Peter's See.

I therefore wish at this time to say farewell to this whole gracious institution which, bearing the eloquent name of Father Agostino Gemelli, makes up an organic part of the Catholic University of Italy, connected with that University's Faculty of Medicine.

At this point I would like to express deep and repeated thanks to so many men and women of Gemelli Polyclinic—and also to the other professors invited to collaborate—to whom I owe so much for the whole duration of these three months, beginning with that tragic evening of May 13. Nevertheless, allow me to postpone for another occasion the adequate expression of all this gratitude.

I wish instead, together with all those who deserve this human gratitude—and also together with all who are listening to me at this moment—to give thanks to God, the Creator and Lord of life, for having saved my life and restored my health through the tireless effort of so many highly qualified and totally dedicated men and women, and through the prayer and sacrifice of innumerable friends, perhaps of the whole world.

In giving thanks for this gift of preserved life and restored health, I wish at this time to express thanks for yet another thing: in fact, it has been granted me in the course of these three months, dear brothers and sisters, to belong to your community: to the community of the sick who are suffering in this hospital—and, as a matter of fact, who constitute in a certain sense a special organism in the Church, in the Mystical Body of Christ. In a special way, according to St. Paul, we can say of them that they fill up in their flesh what is lacking in the suffering of Christ... (cf. Col. 1:24). In the course of these months, it was granted me to belong to this special organism. And for this too I heartily thank you, brothers and sisters, at this moment when I take leave of you and your community.

Certainly there were and are among you many persons whose sufferings, incomparably superior to mine, borne by them with love, bring them much closer to the Crucified Redeemer....

More than once I thought of this, embracing everyone in my prayer as your Bishop...and sometimes I received news of those whom the Lord of life called to Himself during these months....

All this I have experienced, dear brothers and sisters, day by day—and this too I wish to tell you today as I take my leave. I now know better than ever that suffering is a certain dimension of life, in which more than ever the grace of redemption is deeply engrafted in the human heart. And if I wish each of you to be able to leave this hospital restored to health, I no less intensely wish that you will be able to take from here also that deep grafting of the divine life which the grace of suffering brings with it.

Once again, as your Bishop, I bless you with the power received from Christ: in the name of the Father and of the Son and of the Holy Spirit. Amen.

The Church's Commitment To Safeguard the Rights of Disabled Persons

On September 17, 1981, the Holy Father met with a large group of disabled persons from the diocese of Verona and offered the following thoughts to the sick, who were accompanied by their bishop, His Excellency Giuseppe Amari, and their relatives.

1. How can I express the joy that your visit brings me, my dearest brothers and sisters who have come from Verona, led by your bishop, His Excellency Giuseppe Amari, to bring me evidence of your affection and devotion.

I am grateful to you for this gesture of cordial affection which stirs up in my heart a deep and lively echo. I greet you one by one, and with you, besides your relatives, I greet the priests and faithful of the parish communities who have accompanied you and who kindly lend you their assistance. My thought extends likewise to all the other disabled and sick of the diocese of Verona who were not able to join your pilgrimage, but who are certainly present in their affection and with their prayer.

I wish to tell everyone of the high regard with which the Church looks upon your condition and the great esteem she has for the contribution you are able to make toward her activity for the coming of the kingdom of God into the world.

RIGHTS OF THE DISABLED

2. I was pleased to learn that your diocese, in connection with the International Year of the Disabled Person proclaimed by the UN, has scheduled a series of initiatives aimed at promoting the inclusion in social and parochial life of those who are hampered by a certain form of disability.

In expressing my appreciation for this concrete demonstration of human and Christian sensitivity, I wish to reaffirm the inspiring principle of every action of the Church in this field, namely, that the disabled person is a full-fledged human subject whose innate rights remain sacred and inviolable.

Therefore it is right that we promote as much as possible his inclusion in the living fabric of social relationships, since every emargination cannot but negatively mark his human development and the achievement of his potential, often very rich, which bespeaks human development.

The ecclesial community must bear witness by word and deed to this conviction, which is strengthened in her by the light of faith. In fact, faith teaches us to see in every person the image of God, which shines brightly behind the veil that the handicap can spread over you. To the person, therefore, in every case, belongs the primacy over other values, particularly over values of the economic order.

MUTUAL ENRICHMENT AND COMMON GROWTH

3. I am certain that in renewing the traditions of Christian concern for the needy, in which it has always been distinguished, the diocese of Verona will be able to conceive adequate forms of intervention to overcome the isolation in which the disabled persons and their families often seem to be confined. Thanks to the generosity of everyone, isolation will give way to sharing and the result will be a mutual enrichment and a common growth, from which will spring a greater joy for each one.

I hope and trust that today's audience will bring new thrust to the commitment that the whole diocese has taken upon itself in its pastoral area, by arousing in both the disabled and the "healthy" the will to find new forms of encounter and collaboration.

Dearest brothers and sisters, a long road is before you: embark on it confidently. With you walks the Lord, who has willed to identify Himself with every needy and suffering person.

In invoking constant divine assistance upon you and your good intentions, I gladly impart to all of you the conciliatory apostolic blessing, which I extend with all my heart to your relatives and to all the sick that you will find when you return to your parishes. May our Lady accompany you and protect you always.

Before going back inside, the Holy Father paused at the door for a moment and gave this parting message:

I embrace every one of you and your families. I am grateful to you for the gift you have brought here: the gift of your suffering, a gift of sacrifice and prayer. Particularly in these past months we have had a true and real solidarity with the suffering. I recommend myself to your prayers and sacrifices: always, not only today, but for all the days of my life and yours. Again I thank your parishes, the priests, sisters, and families who have brought you here. I want to thank especially the young people, who are so numerous, who sing—and sing well—and who bring real joy to the suffering and to all of us. I thank you again, not only for the suffering and sacrifice that you bear, but also for this joy that you have brought to Castel Gandolfo.

With the Eyes of Faith

On September 29, 1981, the Holy Father celebrated Mass in the chapel at Castel Gandolfo for an inter-diocesan group of Swiss disabled persons who had come to Rome on a pilgrimage (Rom in Rollstuhl —*Rome in a wheelchair). The Holy Father delivered the following homily.*

I greet you heartily, dear brothers and sisters, on your first *Rom in Rollstuhl* pilgrimage from various dioceses of Switzerland. I bid you an equally hearty welcome to this common Eucharistic Celebration of ours.

I met your desire for such a meeting with special joy. It is a welcome opportunity for me to encourage this praiseworthy initiative for disabled persons in Switzerland, which is to be continued also in future years, and to thank all those who in your native country and elsewhere place their strength at the service of disabled persons in a spirit of Christian brotherhood. Above all, however, the Pope would like to express to you yourselves, dear disabled brothers and sisters, his deep sympathy and love, his high esteem and the great confidence he places in you, in your help through prayer and sacrifice—particularly through the patient and self-sacrificing acceptance of your suffering.

Consider your fate in life above all with the eyes of faith. What seems to the unbeliever a tragic misfortune can become for the believer an extremely meaningful and fulfilling role in the midst of the human community and the Church. Our fate is not the result of blind chance, but has been intended or permitted by the loving God, and His quite personal call reaches us in it. From it we recognize the mission and task entrusted to each one of us. Try to grasp yours, which has fallen to your lot through the fate of physical disability, more and more deeply in the light of the cross. Try to accept it, following the suffering Lord, with deep inner readiness, and to make it fruitful for the Church's work of salvation in the world.

At this Eucharistic Celebration and every day anew, unite your trials and sufferings with the redeeming sufferings of Jesus Christ, whereby precisely your life of disability acquires inestimable value in the eyes of God and in the plan of salvation. May today's Mass with the Pope and this pilgrimage to Rome strengthen you in this consoling view of faith and also make your life deeply joyful and happy. This is what I wish and pray for you in this hour of Christ in the Eucharist with my special apostolic blessing.

A Great Divine Trial

In the course of the general audience in St. Peter's Square on October 14, 1981, the Holy Father delivered the following address.

1. Last Wednesday, during the general audience, I referred to the event of May 13. Since that day interrupted the meetings we are now resuming thanks to my recovery, I wish to share with you at least briefly what the content of my meditations was in that period of some months, in which I participated in a great divine trial.

I say a divine trial. Although, in fact, the events of May 13—the attempt on the Pope's life and also its consequences associated with the operation and treatment at the Gemelli Hospital—have their fully human dimension, this, however, cannot dim an even more profound dimension: the dimension, precisely, of the trial permitted by God. All that I spoke to you about last Wednesday must also be set in this dimension. Today I wish to return to it once more.

During the last few months God has allowed me to experience suffering, and to experience the danger of losing my life. At the same time He has allowed me to understand clearly and completely that this is a special grace of His for me myself as a man, and at the same time—considering the service I am carrying out as Bishop of Rome and Successor of St. Peter—a grace for the Church.

CALLED TO BEAR WITNESS

2. And so, dear brothers and sisters, I know that I have experienced a great grace. And recalling with you all that happened on May 13 and in the whole following period, I cannot but speak about this above all. Christ, who is the Light of the world, the Shepherd of His fold, and above all the Prince of pastors, has granted me the grace to be able, through suffering and at the risk of life and health, to bear witness to His Truth and to His Love. It is precisely this that I consider to be a particular grace bestowed on me—and for this reason I express my gratitude especially to the Holy Spirit, whom the Apostles and their successors received on the day of Pentecost as the fruit of the cross and resurrection of their Master and Redeemer.

It is for this reason that, this year, the feast of the descent of the Holy Spirit took on particular significance for me, when, together with the whole Church, and especially in union with the Ecumenical Patriarchate, we gave thanks for the gift of the First Council of Constantinople celebrated 1600 years ago—together with the commemoration, here in Rome, 1550 years afterwards, of the Council of Ephesus. From the time of the First Council of Constantinople the whole Church has professed: "I believe in the Holy Spirit who is the Lord and giver of life."

It was precisely to this Holy Spirit "who gives life" that Christ referred when He said to the Apostles before His ascension to the Father: "You shall receive power when the Holy Spirit has come upon you; and you shall be my witnesses in Jerusalem and in all Judea and Samaria and to the ends of the earth" (Acts 1:8). It was the Holy Spirit who, from the day of Pentecost, helped the Apostles to bear witness first in Jerusalem and then in various countries of the world of that time. It was He who gave them the strength to bear witness to Christ before the whole people, and, when they were going to face torture for this, He allowed them to rejoice "that they were counted worthy to suffer dishonor for the name [of Jesus]" (Acts 5:41).

It was the Holy Spirit who led Paul of Tarsus through the streets of the world of that time. It was the Holy Spirit who sustained Peter in bearing witness to Christ, first in Jerusalem, then in Antioch, and finally here in Rome, the capital of the Empire. This witness was confirmed at the end with martyrdom, as was also the witness of Paul of Tarsus, the great Apostle of the Gentiles.

LIKE HIS PREDECESSORS

3. These words which Christ the Lord and Redeemer, Christ the eternal Pastor of souls, addressed to the Apostles before going to the

Father, refer to their successors, and refer also to all Christians. The Apostles, in fact, are the beginning of the new People of God, as the Council teaches (cf. AG 5). But if all are called to bear witness to the crucified and risen Christ, those after the Apostles who inherited the pastoral and magisterial service in the Church are called in a particular way. How many Successors of Peter in this Roman See have sealed this witness of pastoral and magisterial service with the sacrifice of their life? This is shown by the Sacred Liturgy when, in the course of the year, it recalls the numerous Sovereign Pontiffs who followed Peter in bearing witness with their blood.

It is difficult to speak of these things without deep veneration, without interior anxiety. In fact, from the sacrifice of those who bore witness to the crucified and risen Christ, especially during the first centuries, the Mystical Body of Christ increased, the Church emerged, became more deeply rooted in souls and consolidated in that ancient world which—so often—responded to the Good News of the Gospel with bloody persecutions.

TO STRENGTHEN THE CHURCH

4. All those who come to Rome, to the "apostolic memories," those who return in the footsteps of St. Peter and St. Paul, should keep all this before their eyes. I, too, am a pilgrim here. I am a foreigner, who, by the will of the Church, has had to remain here and assume the succession in the Roman See after so many great Popes,

Bishops of Rome. And I, too, feel my human weakness deeply—and therefore I repeat the Apostle's words confidently: *virtus in infirmitate perficitur*, "My power is made perfect in weakness" (2 Cor. 12:9). And therefore, with deep gratitude to the Holy Spirit, I think of that weakness that He permitted me to experience since May 13, believing and humbly trusting that it may have served for the strengthening of the Church and also that of my human person.

This is the dimension of the divine trial which is not easy to reveal to man. It is not easy to speak of it with human words. Yet it is necessary to speak of it. It is necessary to confess with the deepest humility before God and the Church this great grace, which became my portion at that very period when the whole People of God was preparing for a special celebration of Pentecost, dedicated this year to the memory of the First Council of Constantinople—after 1600 years—and also of the Council of Ephesus—after 1550 years.

In Ephesus there reechoed anew, to the advantage of the whole Church of that time, the truth about Christ—the only-begotten Son of God, who through the work of the Holy Spirit became true Man, conceived in the womb of the Virgin Mary and born of her for the salvation of the world. Mary is therefore the true Mother of God *(Theotokos)*.

So when, dear brothers and sisters, I meditate with you on the grace received with the threat to my life and the suffering, I turn particularly to her: to her whom we also call "Mother of Divine Grace." And I ask that this grace "not be in vain" (cf. 1 Cor. 15:10)—like every grace that man receives: everywhere in any time. I ask that, by means of every grace that the Father, Son and Holy Spirit pour out abundantly, there be born that strength which grows in our weakness. I ask that the witness of truth and love, to which the Lord has called us, also increase and spread.

TO SPECIAL GROUPS

It is a pleasure to greet all the English-speaking visitors and pilgrims, especially the large numbers from England and Scotland, from Ireland and from the United States. At this time I wish to recall how, during the past months, I have been given the grace to bear witness to Christ's truth and His love. In God's Providence I have been able to do this through the suffering that was mine as a result of the attempt on my life. This has indeed turned out to be a special grace for me and for the whole Church. Because of our human weakness we put our trust fully in Christ Jesus. And for all of this I give thanks, together with you, to the Holy Spirit, who is the Lord and Giver of life.

I extend a particular welcome to the members of the New York Section of the American Urological Association. May God enable you to serve humanity well. The numerous Scottish visitors include a pilgrimage commemorating the canonization of St. John Ogilvie. Through his intercession may God's blessings descend abundantly upon Scotland and upon the whole Church.

Forgiveness: a Grace and a Mystery of the Heart

At the general audience in St. Peter's Square on October 21, 1981, the Holy Father continued his reflections on his experiences of May 13 and the subsequent period of convalescence, concentrating on the subject of forgiveness.

1. Again today, at this welcome meeting with you, dear brothers and sisters, I wish to return to the event of last May 13. I return to it to recall what was already spoken on that day before Christ, who is Master and Redeemer of our souls, and what was subsequently said aloud and publicly on the following Sunday, May 17, at the *Regina Caeli.*

Here are the words which today I not only report, but also repeat, to express the truth contained in them, which today just as then is the truth of my soul, of my heart and my conscience:

"Beloved brothers and sisters, I know that during these days and especially in this hour of the *Regina Caeli* you are united with me. With deep emotion I thank you for your prayers and I bless you all. I am particularly close to the two persons wounded together with me. I pray for that brother of ours who shot me, and whom I have sincerely pardoned. United with Christ,

Priest and Victim, I offer my sufferings for the Church and for the world.

"To you, Mary, I repeat: *Totus tuus ego sum* (I belong entirely to you)."

2. Forgiveness! Christ taught us to forgive. He spoke of forgiveness very often and in various ways. When Peter asked Him how often he should forgive his neighbor, "as many as seven times?", Jesus answered that he should forgive "seventy times seven times" (Mt. 18:21f.). That means, in practice, always: in fact, the number "seventy" times "seven" is symbolical, and it means, more than a given quantity, an incalculable, infinite quantity. Answering the question on how we must pray, Christ uttered those magnificent words addressed to the Father: "Our Father who art in heaven"; and among the requests that compose this prayer, the last one speaks of forgiveness: "And forgive us our debts, as we also have forgiven our debtors," those who are guilty towards us ("our debtors"). Finally Christ Himself confirmed the truth of these words on the cross, when, turning to the Father, He begged: "Father, forgive them; for they know not what they do" (Lk. 23:34).

"Forgiveness" is a word spoken by the lips of a man to whom some evil has been done. It is, in fact, the word of the human heart. In this word of the heart each of us endeavors to go beyond the frontier of hostility, which can separate us from the other; he tries to reconstruct the interior space of understanding, contact, bond. Christ taught us with the word of the Gospel, and above all with His own example, that this space opens not only before the other man, but at the same time before God Himself. The Father, who is the God of forgiveness and mercy, wishes to act precisely in this space of human forgiveness—He wishes to forgive those who are capable of forgiving one another, those who try to put into practice those words: "Forgive us...as we forgive."

Forgiveness is a grace which we must consider with deep humility and gratitude. It is a mystery of the human heart, which is difficult to fathom. However, I would like to dwell on what I said. I said it because it is strictly part of the event of May 13 as a whole.

CAIN AND ABEL

3. During the three months that I spent in the hospital, there often came to my mind that passage from the book of Genesis, which we all know well:

"Abel was a keeper of sheep, and Cain a tiller of the ground. In the course of time Cain brought to the Lord an offering of the fruit of the ground, and Abel brought of the firstlings of his flock and of their fat portions. And the Lord had regard for Abel and his offering, but for Cain and his offering he had no regard. So Cain was very angry, and his countenance fell. The Lord said to Cain, 'Why are you angry, and why has your countenance fallen? If you do well, will you not be accepted? And if you do not do well, sin is crouching at the door; its desire is for you, but you must master it.'

"Cain said to Abel his brother, 'Let us go out to the field.' And when they were in the field, Cain rose up against his brother Abel, and killed him. Then the Lord said to Cain, 'Where is Abel your brother?' He said, 'I do not know; am I my brother's keeper?' And the Lord said, 'What have you done? The voice of your brother's blood is crying to me from the ground!...'" (Gn. 4:2-10)

THE "BEGINNING" OF SIN AGAINST MAN'S LIFE

4. This very ancient text, which speaks of man's first attempt on man's life—the brother's attempt on his brother's life—often came to my mind in my meditations in the hospital.

At that time, therefore, when the man who made the attempt on my life was being tried and when he received the sentence, I was thinking of the account of Cain and Abel, which biblically expresses the "beginning" of sin against man's life. In our time, in which this sin against man's life has become threatening again and in a new way, while so many innocent men are perishing at the hands of other men, the biblical description of what happened between Cain and Abel becomes particularly eloquent. Even more complete, even more overwhelming than the commandment itself "You shall not kill." This order belongs to the ten commandments, which Moses received from God and which are at the same time written in man's heart as the interior life of moral order for all human behavior. Does not that question of God addressed to Cain: "Where is your brother?" speak to us even more than the absolute ban "not to kill"? And following up closely on Cain's evasive reply, "Am I my brother's keeper?" comes the other divine question: "What have you done? The voice of your brother's blood is crying to me from the ground!"

CHRIST TAUGHT US FORGIVENESS

5. Christ taught us to forgive. Forgiveness is indispensable also for God to put to human conscience some questions to which He expects an answer in complete interior truth.

At this time, in which so many innocent men are perishing at the hands of other men, there seems to be a special need to approach each of those who kill, approach them with forgiveness in one's heart and at the same time with the same question that God, the Creator and Lord of human life, asked the first man who had made an attempt on his brother's life and had taken it from him—had taken what belongs only to the Creator and Lord of life.

Christ taught us to forgive. He taught Peter to forgive "seventy times seven times" (Mt. 18:22). God Himself forgives when man answers with the whole interior truth of conversion the question addressed to his conscience and to his heart.

Leaving to God Himself the judgment and the sentence in its definitive dimension, let us not cease to ask: "Forgive us our debts as we have forgiven our debtors."

Gratitude to Doctors

Over five months after the tragic attempt in Saint Peter's Square, on November 3, 1981, the Holy Father received in audience the doctors of the Agostino Gemelli Hospital and those of the Medical Services of Vatican City, with the members of their families. After an address of homage to the Pope by Prof. Lazzati of the Catholic University of the Sacred Heart, the Holy Father improvised the following greeting.

I must say that I find myself in a difficult situation because the Rector of the Catholic University spoke from a written sheet, while I find myself before you without any papers. I must find them inside me, for everything that I want to say and must say to you is written in my heart. It is a question of a very simple word, an apostolic word: *Debitores facti sumus* (We were made debtors). I deeply feel in this position and perhaps also the circumstance of the day we have chosen for this informal meeting increases and deepens in me the awareness of being a *debitor*. On the eve of the feast of St. Charles Borromeo, my heavenly patron, I feel I am a *debitor* to my parents, who gave me life and then introduced me to the Church and with the mystery of Baptism introduced me into another life, a superior, divine life. The name Charles is closely connected with that mystery, that benefit, for which I feel I am a *debitor*.

I feel in this same situation, in this same position, before you all, beloved professors and doctors. I see you gathered here on a solemn occasion, but I saw you during those weeks and months in another situation, we can say a situation of work, that most noble work whose object or subject is another man, it was I myself. Once more, then, I wish to express to you the deep consciousness bound up with the Apostle's words, *Debitores facti sumus;* for each of you, gratitude, a simple thank you to each of you. Today, preparing to celebrate the feast of my patron saint, I want to show my grateful remembrance to each of you. A remembrance full of thankfulness for everything you did during those weeks, those months, in that difficult period of my life. I thank divine Providence for the fact that I am still able to be here, in this place, in this hall, on St. Charles' day. I thank Providence and I thank you. You have been instruments of Providence, saving my life, assisting me during my illness and causing me to recover my health with great patience and love. I thank you for this love.

To give our meeting the character of an informal gathering, I will take the liberty of passing among you, from one professor to another, greeting everyone and offering a poor sign of this gratitude of mine and also of the gratitude of the Holy See, the See of Peter, which is, with us, grateful to all the professors and doctors, especially of the Gemelli Hospital, but also of the other universities, other circles and other institutions that helped the Pope in the days between May 13 and, we can say, approximately August 13.

John Paul II then moved among those present and stopped to speak to everyone, conferring medals on some of the eminent physicians. The Pope then returned to the microphone for a last greeting.

Finally, I must say that some persons are missing, above all the sisters and male and female nurses whom I have already met once to thank them too for the service they rendered during my stay in Gemelli Hospital. And I would say that so many other persons who took part in that event are missing. So I want to recall also all those persons who were part of this physical, historical, but above all spiritual team. Returning to the words of the Apostle, *Debitores facti sumus,* I want to repeat once more that I feel indebted to all these people and above all to all those who are present. I thank you and warmly bless you. May God our Father reward you all, your persons, your families and your environment, the Gemelli Hospital, the Catholic University of the Sacred Heart, and the Toniolo Institute; may He reward you abundantly because He is *dives in misericordia.* I would be very happy and grateful to be able to complete this meeting with a gift of my person, my vocation and my ministry by imparting the blessing. Let us pray for all those present, and for all the others who belong to this team of which I have spoken.

The Elderly in the Family

Excerpt from the Apostolic Exhortation on "The Role of the Christian Family in the Modern World," Familiaris consortio, *November 22, 1981, no. 27.*

There are cultures which manifest a unique veneration and great love for the elderly: far from being outcasts from the family or merely tolerated as a useless burden, they continue to be present and to take an active and responsible part in family life, though having to respect the autonomy of the new family; above all they carry out the important mission of being a witness to the past and a source of wisdom for the young and for the future.

Other cultures, however, especially in the wake of disordered industrial and urban development, have both in the past and in the present set the elderly aside in unacceptable ways. This causes acute suffering to them and spiritually impoverishes many families.

The pastoral activity of the Church must help everyone to discover and to make good use of the role of the elderly within the civil and ecclesial community, in particular within the family. In fact, "the life of the aging helps to clarify a scale of human values; it shows the continuity of generations and marvelously demonstrates the interdependence of God's people. The elderly often have the charism to bridge generation gaps before they are made: how many children have found understanding and love in the eyes and words and caresses of the aging! And how many old people have willingly subscribed to the inspired word that the 'crown of the aged is their children's children'!" (Prv. 17:6) (John Paul II, Address to the participants in the International Forum on Active Aging [September 5, 1980], 5: *Insegnamenti di Giovanni Paolo II,* III, 2 [1980], 539)

Acceptance of Suffering for the Victory of Good over Evil

After individually greeting all the sick, John Paul delivered the following address to the group assembled in the Sanctuary of Merciful Love, Collevalenza, November 22, 1981.

Dear brothers and sisters in the Lord!

1. It is with particular emotion that I address you at this moment which was supposed to precede the celebration of Holy Mass at this Sanctuary of Merciful Love, but has come after. I wish to express to you, in the first place, my affection, to manifest to you my appreciation and exhort you to persevere courageously along the difficult way on which you have been placed by God's Providence which, if it often seems mysterious in its plans, is, however, always moved by infinitely wise and considerate love.

References to the meetings of Jesus with sick persons are frequent in the Gospel. He did not remain indifferent before any situation of human suffering, but had for them all a gesture of help and a word of comfort. This attitude of His was transferred to the Church, which learned from Him to love the sick and endeavor to bring to them, together with the illuminating word of faith, the concrete help that circumstances made possible.

2. You understand, therefore, why the Pope wishes to meet those who are suffering and feels it his particular duty to bring to each one the renewed proof of God's love and the fervent call to revive hope. Suffering, since Christ took it upon Himself, has assumed an inestimable value: it has become a source of saving energy for the person who bears it and for the whole of mankind.

Allow me, therefore, to tell you too that I am relying a great deal on the contribution you can make to the cause of the kingdom of Christ in the world. The liturgy calls us today to meditate on the nature and on the destiny of this kingdom. Well, as you know, Jesus did not conquer it by force, nor did He entrust its future to the violence of arms. *Regnavit a ligno Deus*—God reigned from the cross!

It was with suffering and death that Jesus conquered the forces of evil, reversing the desperate situation in which humanity found itself and winning for every child of Adam the right to be a citizen of that kingdom of love and freedom which, announced here below in the Church, will have its full realization in heaven.

3. Christ's death on the cross marked human history forever: now, in the dramatic conflict between good and evil, of which human history is the stage and the witness, the most valuable contribution to the assertion of the forces of good can be made only by suffering accepted and offered in loving communion with the Son of God, who renews on the altar the supreme sacrifice carried out "once for all" on Golgotha.

How could we not reflect on this mysterious and fascinating dimension of human participation in redemption, now that we are about to begin the celebration of the Eucharist, in which Jesus will be among us again in the reality of His pasch of death and resurrection?

Give me your sufferings, brothers and sisters! I will take them to the altar, to offer them to God the Father in union with those of His only-begotten Son and to implore, also in their name, peace for the Church, mutual understanding among nations, the humility of repentance for those who have sinned, the generosity of forgiveness for those who have been offended, and for everyone the joy of a renewed experience of God's merciful love. May the Blessed Virgin, who "was standing by the cross of Jesus" (cf. Jn. 19:25) while He was dying for us, arouse in our hearts appropriate sentiments for this hour of light and grace. Amen.

Complete Dedication to the Defense of Health and Human Life

On December 20, 1981, the Holy Father paid a visit to the new Regina Margherita Hospital in Trastevere. In the course of the visit, he delivered the following address.

Beloved brothers and sisters!

1. On my visit to the Regina Margherita Hospital, I wish in the first place to extend my cordial, respectful greeting to the directors, doctors, personnel and sisters, and to all who are here for this meeting. To all of you I express my esteem and consideration for the irreplaceable work of real human advancement and of admirable social value which you carry out in the exercise of your duty, or rather, of your mission.

But my particularly affectionate thought cannot but be directed to the dear patients in this institute, stricken by illness. To you who are suffering in body and in spirit, there go my good wishes, my understanding, and my solidarity, which I intend to manifest also to your relatives here present, who are deeply concerned and anxious about your health.

I come to this hospital complex which was restructured and inaugurated in 1970. However, going back in the history of Rome, it is connected with the monastery of San Cosimato, which from the 10th century was a center of fervent religious life and also of generous charitable undertakings, particularly in favor of the sick and pilgrims, a concrete sign of that continuous, active and disinterested solicitude that the Church has always shown for the poor, the humble, children and the sick.

SUFFERING AND HOPE

2. This hospital—like all the hospitals of the world—is a place of suffering and of hope. As we enter the wards, the rooms, we dramatically experience the weakness, the frailty of our human nature, so exposed to a thousand dangers and threats, which can at any moment break its harmonious balance, causing disease and weakening our strength. The mystery of physical pain, which torments man's spirit in one of the most agonizing questions, appears here with all its intense impact. In suffering, man feels his loneliness become more acute, while his physical strength fails him; the need of invoking others—relatives, friends, doctors—to give him relief and comfort; the cry of supplication to God, who alone can give complete help and also explain the meaning of so much suffering.

But this place is also a place of hope: the hope of the sick themselves, who feel that the beauty of life is insuppressible; the hope of their relatives and friends, who share with them the confident expectation of an improvement which will announce recovery in the near future.

While I express my wish that this hope will soon come true, I wish to say to the brothers and sisters stricken by sickness, who are listening to me at this moment: I have come to bear witness to the love that Christ, the Church and the Pope have for you. Your suffering presence is not useless, far less absurd. Christ the Lord, who in the Incarnation assumed, along with our human nature, also pain and death, calls all men, and especially you who are weak and suffering, to collaborate with Him for the salvation of the world. This mysterious vocation of yours to suffering is a vocation to love: for God the Father of Mercy, and for others, brothers and sisters. Only Christ's cross can illuminate our weak intelligence and give it a glimpse of the deep meaning of the human and Christian fruitfulness of suffering.

IN DEFENSE OF HEALTH AND HUMAN LIFE

3. A place of suffering which is accompanied by hope, a hospital is also a place in which an effort is made to make this hope become a reality as soon as possible. Medical activity by its very nature is directed to defending life and improving the health of any human being in difficulty. The very ancient Hippocratic Oath already committed physicians to do so. In a central passage, it ran: "I will have recourse to diet for the benefit of my patients according to my capacities and judgment, not for their danger and harm. And I will not give a deadly potion, nor will I take a similar initiative, whoever may ask me; in the same way I will not give any woman a pessary for abortive purposes."

Twenty-four centuries later, the "Geneva Declaration," approved in 1948 by the World

Association of Doctors, proposes substantially identical concepts. In it the one who assumes practice of the medical profession promises: "I solemnly undertake to dedicate my life to the service of humanity.... I will practice my profession with conscientiousness and dignity. The health of my patient will be my first concern.... I will maintain the utmost respect for human life right from the moment of conception."

It is precisely this unreserved dedication to the defense of health and human life that is the origin of the special consideration universally attributed by citizens to doctors and auxiliary personnel: while respecting all other work, everyone willingly recognizes the social preeminence of a profession which has as its aim the protection of a good, which is the foundation and premise of all other goods that can be enjoyed here below.

And it is holy Scripture itself that confirms this appreciation, recommending: "Honor the physician with the honor due him, according to your need of him" (Sir. 38:1), and commenting on this precept, it observes: "The skill of the physician lifts up his head, and in the presence of great men he is admired" *(ibid.,* v. 3).

Certainly, for the believer the first and main source of hope, in the case of illness, remains the help of the Lord, whose omnipotence can triumph over any disease. For this reason the page of the Bible quoted urges the sick to pray, to be purified and to offer propitiating sacrifices (cf. *ibid.*, vv. 9-11). That does not exclude, however, the opportuneness of simultaneous recourse to the aids of the medical art, whose beneficial function is also envisaged in the plans of divine Providence. For this reason, after the admonitions just recalled, Scripture does not fail to recommend: "Give the physician his place, for the Lord created him; let him not leave you, for there is need of him" *(ibid.*, v. 12).

PRECIOUS HUMAN LIFE

4. It is only right, therefore, that your profession, beloved doctors and members of the paramedical and auxiliary personnel, should be held in high consideration. It is only right, because the good that it intends to protect, the good of human life, is a highly precious one.

Life is the time that is granted to us to express concretely the potential riches which each of us bears and to make our contribution to the common progress of mankind. Life is the time that is given to us to embody in ourselves and in history the values of love, goodness, joy, justice and peace, to which the human heart aspires.

In the light of faith, furthermore, life is the time of grace *(kairos)*, in which God puts the human being to the test, trying his heart and his mind by the daily commitment of believing, hoping and loving. A time of grace, in which each one is called to enrich himself—by giving himself—with values that last for eternity, which will be marked forever by the measure of love which we have succeeded in expressing here below.

Life, therefore, is a precious good, in its entirety and in every part. Those who spend their energies to defend it, to restore its normal efficiency, to promote its full development, acquire the right to the gratitude of every fellow creature of theirs. On the contrary, those who dare to attack it in any way stain themselves with a serious crime and incur the severe condemnation of that judge against which there is no appeal: conscience, the mirror of God.

The hope that I spontaneously express on the occasion of this significant meeting is that, also today, anyone who chooses to put himself in the service of human life will feel vibrating in him pride in belonging to a profession whose members, throughout the centuries, have offered luminous testimonies of generous humanitarianism, reaching, in some cases, the supreme heroism of self-sacrifice to save their brother.

May the thought of Christmas, which we are preparing to celebrate, strengthen these wishes with the attraction that springs from the smile of a newborn child in his mother's arms. The inspiring scene, which we will contemplate represented in the crib, speaks to us all of a life that has just been born, which the warmth and solicitude of loving hearts (of Mary, Joseph, the shepherds) defend from the dangers of a difficult situation.

May this message bring forth echoes of generous response in the hearts of Christians today, so that every human life may find around it, not indifference or rejection, but sympathy, welcome, interest and help. This is my cordial wish, which I accompany with the apostolic blessing, imploring so much serenity for you and for your dear ones.

Irreplaceable Role of the Elderly in the Family and in Society

On January 3, 1982, more than fifty thousand faithful gathered in St. Peter's Square to pray the Angelus *with the Holy Father, who invited everyone to turn their thoughts to the elderly, that vast portion of the human family that society increasingly sets aside and forgets. The following is the text of Pope John Paul's message.*

1. Today, dear brothers and sisters, I want our thoughts and our hearts to turn to elderly people. Christmas time puts before our eyes the figures of Simeon and Anna, who welcomed Emmanuel in the Temple of Jerusalem. They had waited for Him in the long advent of their whole life, and had the fortune of seeing Him at the end of the days of their earthly existence.

How eloquent are Simeon's words:

"Lord, now let your servant depart in peace
according to your word;
For my eyes have seen your salvation
which you have prepared in the presence of
all the peoples,
A light for revelation to the Gentiles,
and for the glory to your people Israel" (Lk. 2:29-32).

Among the words that have been spoken about Christ, these are particularly striking. They are inspired by the faith of a long expectation, but also by a great wisdom characteristic of advanced age.

Anna, also called "prophetess" in the Gospel, although she was eighty-four years old, "did not depart from the temple, worshiping with fasting and prayer day and night" (Lk. 2:37).

2. Let these two splendid testimonies linked with the Christmas period form our meditation and prayer today.

The Church wishes to make her voice heard in support of elderly people, so well-deserving, but sometimes also so disregarded. So I repeat to you today what I had to say in November 1980, in Munich's Cathedral: "The Pope respectfully bows before the elderly and calls upon everyone to do so with him. Old age is a crowning of the stages of life. It bears the harvest of what has been learned and lived, the harvest of what has been carried out and reached, the harvest of what has been suffered and borne. As at the end of a great symphony, the dominant themes of life return for a powerful synthesis in sound. And this conclusive resonance confers wisdom...goodness, patience, understanding: love" (no. 1).

The old, therefore, are extremely precious, and I would say indispensable, for the family and for society. How much help they are to young parents and their children with their knowledge and experience! Their advise and their action also benefit so many groups, in which they, too, have their places, and so many initiatives in the sphere of ecclesial and civil life. Let us all be grateful for this!

3. But they too, in their turn, need to be sustained and comforted in the difficulties in which they may find themselves because of health and

loneliness. I express deep appreciation to all those persons who find the time and the way to approach and assist the elderly who are in most need because they are abandoned or forgotten in homes for the aged, which sometimes lack human warmth.

In particular, I address a thought of gratitude and encouragement to the young who dedicate themselves to spiritual and social assistance of the aged. It is a question of initiatives taken either by individuals or by movements and organized associations, inspired by Christian faith which makes us see the face of Jesus Himself under the face of the person in need.

To all these young people, I again express today my appreciation, my affection and, blessing them, I hope that they will continue in this meritorious and noble work of theirs.

"To Jesus Through Mary" Must Be Made True Also for Us

In the Vatican Basilica on February 11, 1982, the liturgical commemoration of Our Lady of Lourdes, the Holy Father presided at a concelebrated Mass for the sick, who were assisted by UNITALSI and pilgrims of the Roman Pilgrimage Organization. Pope John Paul delivered the following homily.

Benedicta tu inter mulieres! (Blessed are you among women!) (Lk. 1:42)

1. This eloquent greeting to Mary—which repeats and echoes throughout the centuries

the greeting that Elizabeth, "filled with the Holy Spirit...in a loud voice" (cf. *ibid.*, vs. 41-42) addressed to the Virgin Mother of God—seems to me, dearest brothers and sisters, particularly appropriate for this evening's welcome liturgical assembly. In fact, we have assembled inside this temple to honor and celebrate Mary most holy on the day that recalls her apparition to lowly Bernadette in that grotto of Massabielle to entrust to her a special message of mercy and grace. And who could say that such a message does not retain its full value even for our days?

Availing herself of that unknown little girl, Mary intended above all to call sinners to conversion, soliciting for them and their salvation the common commitment of all faithful Christians. As a matter of fact, this appeal—as the Liturgy of the Hours stresses in a brief introductory note to today's memorial—"aroused in the Church a fervent movement of prayer and charity, above all in service of the sick and the poor."

AN IRREPLACEABLE ROLE RESERVED FOR YOU

2. This is just what we intend to do this evening! Gathering you together for the celebration of the Eucharist, which is the sacrament of piety and the bond of charity, I wanted in front of me in an especially principal position so many brothers and sisters tried by pain and suffering. In the light of the ever pertinent message of the Virgin of Lourdes, you are here in front, dearest sick, because an irreplaceable role is reserved for

you in the economy of salvation, in union with Him who with His passion, death, and resurrection is its protagonist and artisan, Jesus Christ, our Lord and Redeemer.

Therefore, after the greeting I addressed to Mary, I now direct to you my affectionate thought, which is both an expression of my good wishes for your health and a sign of gratitude for your presence, which I know is not without its difficulties and sacrifices. Nor can I fail to greet with you all those who, as they have attentively accompanied you here, offer you their fraternal and greatly meritorious "ministry" of assistance and care on so many numerous occasions. Indeed I wish to greet and thank you also, dear directors and members of the National UNITALSI Association and the Roman Pilgrimage Organization, whose assiduous, discreet, disinterested and generous work I know and appreciate. Not only today but daily you perform a work that beyond every limiting sociological or professional qualification has a name that is well defined and honored in the Christian vocabulary: *charity*, as the exercise of evangelical solicitude for the weakest brethren, a solicitude that is offered in the name of God and Jesus His Son. *Infirmus (eram), et visitastis me* (Mt. 25:36). Thank you, also in the name of those who at times do not have the voice or the strength to say it to you.

THE LOFTY LESSON OF THE *MAGNIFICAT*

3. *Benedicta tu inter mulieres!* The greeting that we address to Mary to honor her on

this feast of hers, repeating the "inspired" words of Elizabeth, would not be complete if it were not followed by, and made one with, the other words which, as the Gospel tells us, were uttered with them in Zachary's house. As Elizabeth immediately added, without in any way separating the Mother from the Son, but rather intimately associating them, *et benedictus fructus ventris tui*, so we too must address ourselves to Jesus the Lord with the promptness of a living faith, with the strength of a burning love. For us too there must be shown true, that is, there must be really verified, the content of the expression *ad Iesum per Mariam*, so that today's liturgical observance may also be an occasion and a way to approach Jesus more closely, confessing Him as the "blessed fruit of Mary's womb."

Let us reflect: What did Mary's presence in that house in the hill country of Judah (cf. Lk. 1:39) mean? Was it only a kind act, or a gentle caring for the "kinswoman who had conceived in her old age" (cf. *ibid.*, 1:36)? Was it a purely human act of assistance? No: it was a presence that was most significant and spiritually fruitful, because Mary brought to her cousin the incomparable gifts of grace, joy and light, associating the future precursor in this generous gift to his mother. In fact, when the old woman "no sooner heard Mary's greeting," not only did she feel her child leap in her womb, but she was filled with the Holy Spirit and felt comforted and, I would say, enthusiastic in returning the greeting. And that is not enough: she above all obtained, through the illumination of that Spirit that had entered her, the superior capacity to recognize in this young cousin of hers the Mother of her Lord herself.

These are choicest gifts that Mary, the Mother of Divine Grace, obtains also for us, while she brings us to Jesus, or better—properly speaking—she brings Jesus to us. We must therefore welcome her, as Elizabeth welcomed her.

MARY ALSO BRINGS JESUS TO US

4. The Gospel we have just heard, in addition to the details of the meeting, tells us also what Mary's response then was. Called blessed together with the "fruit of your womb," called "happy for believing" (Lk. 1:45), she indeed answers, but addressing someone else, because she begins speaking to the Lord, raising to Him in her "humility of a servant" a wonderful hymn of praise. The *Magnificat*, true canticle of canticles in the New Testament, daily resounds on our lips, brothers and sisters; but let us be careful to intone it with special fervor in our daily situation, that in spiritual union with Mary, repeating it with her, word for word and almost syllable for syllable, we may learn in her school how and why we must celebrate and bless the Lord.

It teaches us that God alone is great and therefore must be magnified by us; He alone saves us and therefore our spirit must rejoice in Him. He stoops to us with His mercy and raises us to Himself with His power. Great indeed, and lofty, is the lesson of the *Magnificat*, which each one of us, in all life's situations, can and must make our own, to obtain from it, besides those gifts of grace and light, comfort and serenity even in the trial of tribulations and in bodily sufferings themselves. May it be also for you, brothers and sisters who are ill, a source of consolation and peace and may it sustain you in your prayers and in the offering of your sufferings.

ACCOMPANY ME WITH YOUR PRAYERS

5. But this evening I have a special intention to propose to you and a particular request to make of you. As you certainly know, tomorrow I will leave Rome for a few days and, God willing, I will pay a visit to some African countries. This new journey will be like a return trip, because the Lord has already granted me, in May of 1980, to visit a few lands in that great and promising continent. This time I will go to Nigeria, Benin, Gabon, and Equatorial Guinea, and so have the opportunity to meet the numerous ecclesial communities that, thanks to the tireless work of so many generations of well-deserving missionaries, are established there. A missionary journey, precisely because it is directed to these young Churches and because to undertake this journey is a unique service in the cause of the Gospel, in direct contact with the faithful and the pastors of these Churches.

And this is precisely where the request I mentioned comes in: that my upcoming journey may achieve this apostolic goal, I invite you to pray for me! Be willing to accompany me, all you brothers and sisters who are listening to me, with your thought and affection, but above all with the charity of a special prayer that the Lord, who alone can grant it, will give me His indispensable help: it is God who gives the increase! (cf. 1 Cor. 3:6-7) He who suggested this initiative to me will also be willing, thanks to your prayers, to accompany and sustain it, that the "confirming" which, by virtue of the mandate of Peter's Successor, I must give my confreres in the episcopate (cf. Lk. 22:32) may be effective, and the word of exhortation that will reach those Christian communities will be stimulating.

You especially, you who are tried by sickness, be willing to unite the offering of your sufferings and so follow me closely during this journey. You can do very much for me; once again you are in a position to communicate to me that strength which I already mentioned on the day after my election to the See of Rome and whose interior power I also experienced during the period of my sickness.

I know well that this time also I will not be lacking the comfort of your prayers nor the merit of your sufferings, and I want to thank you right now for all of this. During the Holy Sacrifice I will not fail on my part, in union with the charity that is like the life-breath of the Church, to pray for you and your health. Amen.

A Christian Sees Meaning in Suffering

The Pope concluded his visit to Onitsha on February 13, 1982, with a visit to the sick and aged people who had gathered in the courtyard of St. Charles Borromeo Hospital. He spoke to them as follows.

Dear friends,

I am happy to be with you this afternoon, you, the sick and the old. You are precious in the eyes of God. Your lives have a deep meaning for society and for me. My joy is all the greater because I am meeting you in this famous hospital named after St. Charles Borromeo, whose name was given to me by my parents at Baptism. My Predecessor Paul VI visited this place in 1962 when it was at the building stage, and he contributed to its construction. I can see the loving gesture of the Church in Onitsha in naming this hospital after St. Charles Borromeo, the apostle of Milan and the patron of your first archbishop of Onitsha, Charles Heerey, C.S.Sp., who departed from this life in 1967.

1. As long as we are on our earthly pilgrimage, *suffering and sickness will exist.* They are a part of our human condition, and ultimately they are the results of original sin, but they are not necessarily the fault of the individual. There are many people of different ages who suffer through no fault of their own. Children, in particular, are vulnerable to suffering, often caused by the thoughtlessness or negligence of adults. The

reality of sickness and malnutrition in the lives of millions of children is a fact that calls for attention and action. And the condition of the retarded child makes us think about the very meaning of human life. Old age too brings its own difficulties and physical weakness.

2. Although God allows suffering to exist in the world, He does not enjoy it. Indeed, our Lord Jesus Christ, the Son of God made man, *loved the sick;* He devoted a great part of His earthly ministry to healing the sick and comforting the afflicted. Our God is a God of compassion and consolation. And He expects us to take the ordinary means to prevent, relieve and remove suffering and sickness. Therefore we have preventive health care programs; we have doctors, nurses, paramedics, and medical institutions of many kinds. Medical science has made much progress. We should take advantage of all this.

3. But even after all these efforts, suffering and sickness still exist. A Christian sees *meaning in suffering.* He bears such suffering with patience, love of God, and generosity. He offers it all to God, through Christ, especially during the Sacrifice of the Mass. When the sick person receives Holy Communion he unites himself with Christ the Victim. When suffering is associated with Christ's passion and redemptive death, then it has great value for the individual, for the Church and for society. This is the meaning of those wonderful words of St. Paul on which we must meditate over and over again: "Now I rejoice in my sufferings for your sake, and in my flesh I

complete what is lacking in Christ's afflictions for the sake of his body, that is, the Church" (Col. 1:24).

I also know personally what it means to be sick and to stay in the hospital for a long time, and how it is possible to comfort and support others who share the same lot of confinement and suffering, and how necessary it is to pray for the sick and to show them one's loving concern. In this connection, I am happy to note that you have in this hospital a beautiful chapel with the Blessed Sacrament reserved, and that there is a resident chaplain. Jesus Himself wants to be your consolation and strength, through His Eucharistic presence and through the ministry of His priests.

4. You who are advanced in age are senior citizens. You have borne the heat of the day in life's struggle and have gathered much knowledge, wisdom and experience. Please share these generously with the younger generation. You have something very important to offer to the world; and your contribution is purified and enriched through the patience and love that are yours, when you are united with Christ. Old age slows down the body and brings weakness and sometimes sickness. Our response includes medical attention and Christian patience. In union with Christ you are called to thank God the Father for having given you human life and for having called you to live both in this world and forever in union with Christ.

5. In Nigeria you have the beautiful cultural value of the extended family system. The sick

and the old are not abandoned by their children, their nephews and nieces, their cousins or other kindred. The wide umbrella of charity has a roof for all. This is a precious heritage that must be maintained. This ideal is under pressure, especially in the cities and towns, where the old are sometimes cut off from the extended family. The abandonment and solitude of the old results when a great cultural value has been taken away and has been replaced by something totally un-African.

6. To the doctors, the nurses, the paramedics and all others who care for the sick in Nigeria, not forgetting the various medical and nursing councils, professional and administrative, I express my esteem and gratitude. Your humanitarian concern is worthy of great praise. Your Christian charity merits everlasting life. Jesus Himself made concern for the sick something on which our judgment and eternal reward depend: "Come, O blessed of my Father, inherit the kingdom prepared for you from the foundation of the world; for...I was sick and you visited me" (Mt. 25:34, 36).

Humanize Medicine Through Love for the Sick

On February 25, 1982, in the Clementine Hall, the Holy Father gave an audience to the participants of the Second International Course-Congress on "Radio-Diagnostics and Integrated Therapies in Oncology," organized in Rome by the Faculty of Medicine and Surgery of the Catholic University of the Sacred Heart. Pope John Paul addressed the group as follows.

Dear brothers and sisters!

1. I am truly happy to extend my most cordial greetings to all of you who are currently attending the Second International Course-Congress on the theme, "Radiodiagnostics and Integrated Therapies in Oncology," organized by the Faculty of Medicine and Surgery of the Catholic University of the Sacred Heart here in Rome. Looking through the program of the course I noticed that the distinguished speakers come not only from Italy but also from Yugoslavia, Germany, France, England, Canada, the U.S.A. and Japan. We thus have here a representation that is truly widespread and above all qualified in this field in which your competence is fully acknowledged. And thus to all of you, but first of all to the Director of the Course, Professor Attilio Romanini, I renew my greetings expressing my sincere joy in being able to meet you. Further, I thank you for the opportunity that has been afforded me to address myself to an important subject that you have discussed within a field where I must remain your pupil. It is a unique pleasure to be able

to deal frankly with you on the human problem of those suffering from tumors, and to assure you of my encouragement in your invaluable efforts.

RELATIONSHIP WITH THE PATIENT

2. Beyond the strictly technical aspects of the matter, proper to oncology, there always arises, not only for relatives but especially for the doctor, the question of the best relationship to establish with the patient. The illness of cancer indeed remains for the greater part a mystery, both to the public and even to you who are specialists in the subject. This is true both of its origin and its treatment. You are well aware that a psychological breakdown of the patient, especially due to the terrifying or unknown prospects that lie ahead, easily takes place. Expensive or downright crippling treatment, isolation and rejection by the healthy, anguished concern regarding the outcome of the illness are all reasons why, apart from physical pain, this illness is one of the greatest forms of suffering. But at the same time, and considering the matter from another point of view, these are also the reasons why the patient should not be left to himself, but should have his fate become our concern. We should give him faith, we should keep him company, I should say with a fraternal empathy, along the path of his physical and psychological suffering. And all this is required not only of his relatives, who more closely share his anguish, but also and in a particular way it is required of you, the doctors in charge, to say nothing of the nursing staff and the entire therapy team.

DIGNITY OF THE HUMAN PERSON

3. Since it is part of the tradition of the Church to consider as Christian all that is in the fullest sense human, I feel compelled to call upon you now to humanize still more the medicine that you practice, and to establish a link of pure human solidarity with your patients, one which goes beyond a purely professional relationship. Secretly, the patient expects even this from you. Indeed he is before you in all his nobility as a human person who, although in need, suffering and perhaps also disabled, should not for this reason be seen as a passive object, nor as an object of more or less experimental treatment. On the contrary, a person is always a subject and should be treated as such. Herein lies the primary dignity of man. It is precisely in our relationship with a man who suffers, still more so if he is suffering from a tumor, that we find ourselves confronted with a test, one that challenges and puts on trial the existence and the authenticity of our conviction in the matter.

A person by his very nature requires a personal relationship. The patient too is never simply a clinical case, but is always a "man who is ill." He expects competent and efficient treatment, but also the capacity and the art of instilling in him faith even to the point of discussing his condition with him honestly, and above all of adopting a sincere attitude of sympathy, in the etymological sense of the word, so as to put into practice the words of the Apostle Paul which already echo those of an ancient sage: "Rejoice with those who rejoice, weep with those who weep" (Rom. 12:15; cf. Sir. 7:34).

ENCOURAGEMENT IN YOUR NOBLE WORK

4. In this sense, as is clear, the work of the doctor is more of a mission than a mere profession. In fact, his whole humanity is involved and total dedication is required of him. So, dear brothers and sisters, I feel it my duty to encourage you with all my heart in your noble work, both in scientific research and in caring for the sick. Certainly many people owe you a great deal. And, if I may, I will be the spokesman for those who perhaps do not have the opportunity to express it to you themselves, offering you the thanks of all those who suffer from oncological illness. I thank you not only on their behalf, but also on behalf of man in general, for the good that you do them in this area that is so pressing and so tragic.

Carry on, therefore, in your praiseworthy task with tenacity and enthusiasm, according to your respective areas of specialization. I wish each of these to be as fruitful as possible, as is deserving the commitment of your work and the very cause of man himself who, even on the physical level, still awaits the chance to "obtain the glorious liberty of the children of God" (Rom. 8:21).

On my part I can assure you of a particular remembrance in my prayers, that the Lord, who in the definition of the Bible is one who "loves the living" (Wis. 11:26), bless your work and assist your endeavors. As a token of these wishes and as a sign of my deep esteem, I am happy to impart the apostolic blessing to you and to all those who are dear to you.

Suffering Permits Greater Purification in the Mystery of the Cross of Christ

Some 2,500 pilgrims were received in audience by Pope John Paul on March 27, 1982, in the Paul VI Hall. The group, of which about 300 were sick persons confined to wheelchairs or stretchers, was organized by OFTAL, an organization which provides means of transport of the sick to Lourdes and which this year commemorates the fiftieth year of its existence. Some hundred old people were also present. The Holy Father spoke to the group as follows.

Reverend brothers in the Episcopate, and all you who belong to the Federation for Transport of the Sick to Lourdes!

1. I am happy to receive you in this special audience on the occasion of your pilgrimage to Rome which recalls the fiftieth anniversary of your well-deserving organization. I express to you my pleasure and keen interest in this activity planned to bring comfort and human Christian assistance to the sick of your diocesan communities of Vercelli, Acqui, Albenga, Alessandria, Aosta, Biella, Casale, Milan, Novara, Nuoro, Pontremoli, Torino, Tortona and Vigevano.

In taking cognizance of the principal stages of this organization, I have seen that in these fifty years of existence, it has taken as its goal "wise and loving care to give to its compassionate journeys a truly religious character, achieved through prayer, by lovingly assisting the sick and especially by enlightened and trustful devotion to the most holy Virgin," as it was so well expressed in 1959 by the then Archbishop of Milan, Cardinal Montini, in a letter of official approval of OFTAL.

MARVELOUS GROWTH

2. Your organization, in fact, founded in 1932, on the initiative of the late Monsignor Alessandro Rastelli, has marked a marvelous growth in service to the sick through evangelical dedication by bishops, priests, stretcher-bearers and nurses, who each year accompany thousands of their suffering brothers and sisters to the feet of the most holy Virgin at Lourdes, at Banneux, at Oropa and at Loreto. I am moved to learn that just in the April-October period last year, you transported to these Marian shrines some ten thousand sick persons, accompanied by ten bishops, and a very large number of priests, stretcher-bearers, nurses, doctors, pharmacists —and that from your foundation until now you have transported some 300,000 persons. These figures themselves tell of the zeal that animates your charity and inflames your hearts, revealing consequently a clear witness of ecclesial life lived in the fullness of love and

fervent prayer. I view this with satisfaction and willingly take this occasion to encourage you to continue well in this highly meritorious work.

"I was sick and you visited me" (Mt. 25:26) the Lord will one day say to you. May this hope, rather this certainty, sustain you always, but especially in the difficulties you may meet in the endeavor to provide an ever more efficient service. Learn to offer on behalf of the sick your time, energies and human and exterior attitudes, and above all, with such interior sentiments as to create around the sick a cheerful and comforting atmosphere of serenity, peace and joy, and to make them perceive the joy that belongs to brothers who live together and in communion with "the Father of mercies and God of all comfort, who comforts us in our afflictions, so that we may be able to comfort those who are in any affliction" (2 Cor. 1:3-4).

3. This meeting is especially dear to me because of the significant presence of some three hundred sick persons whom you have brought here knowing it would please me; but even more pleasing is the gift of their suffering, which they bring me in person.

Dear sick persons, you can well imagine with what reverence I turn to you, and how much I would like to have at my disposition a long time to spend with you! I assure you that I will not cease to pray for each and all of you, so that this journey may bring great comfort not only to your souls but also to your suffering bodies. I hope that your coming to this center of Christianity will increase your faith, give vigor to your spirit and merit to your suffering.

On your part, always realize that your condition makes you participate more directly in the mystery of the cross, which during the coming Holy Week will be hailed as our "only hope" and as "the scales of the great ransom." For this you can and should offer to Christ your contribution for the salvation of the world.

4. I wish to extend a particularly affectionate greeting to the group of old people who are cared for in the Villa Lazzaroni, in the ninth circumscription of Rome.

Dearest ones, I thank you for your presence and express the wish that you may be able to pass your days, so propitious for prayer and reflection on the truths of faith, in serenity and peace. May your home always be an oasis of tranquillity in which there reigns mutual respect and cordial collaboration composed of little things which can make your lives happy and the burden of years lighter.

To all of you, to those who help and to those who are cared for, I open my heart and express my good will which I wish to strengthen with the apostolic blessing that I now impart to you and to all who provide you with spiritual and material aid and support.

You Are Precious and Irreplaceable Members of Society and the Church

On March 28, 1982, Pope John Paul visited the Don Guanella Institution on Via Aurelia Antica, in Italy, a home which cares for the physically and mentally handicapped. The Holy Father delivered the following message to the "parishioners" of Don Guanella.

Dearest brothers and sisters in the Lord!

1. On this Fifth Sunday of Lent, it is with deep emotion that I find myself here among you, in this place so humanly marked by suffering and yet, in the light of Christian faith, so privileged and spiritually rich. This too is a pastoral visit that I am making, as I do every Sunday possible, to a sector of the vast diocese of Rome; this home too can be called a "parish," a truly very special one in which, instead of the frenzied bustling of the world, there is found the hidden flow of pain, patience and confidence. But you too, the sick and the people who care for you, are very lively and precious citizens, irreplaceable members of the faithful in the fiber of society and the Church; you are effective members of the Body of Christ!

I therefore very gladly accepted the invitation to visit this great and edifying work, named after Blessed Luigi Guanella, the genius of charity who, following the impulse of his spirit which was deeply sensitive to human suffering, and the vocation clearly inspired by God, worked so well and, through his institutions, still continues to work in Rome, in Italy, and beyond.

I therefore wish to address my thanks, along with my most cordial greeting, to Cardinal Ugo Poletti, Vicar General for the city and district of Rome; to Auxiliary Bishop Fiorenzo Angelini, Delegate for the apostolate in hospitals and clinics; to Fr. Tito Credaro, Provincial Superior of the Congregation of the Servants of Charity of the Work of Don Guanella; to Fr. Domenico Saginario, Director of the Theological Seminary; and to Fr. Pietro Ferrari, Director of the Saint Joseph Home.

I then greet with equal respect and cordiality the other authorities who have wished to attend this ceremony, the doctors and paramedic personnel, the therapists and the various technicians, who with love and skill dedicate their time to the handicapped. I also address my fatherly greeting to the relatives, to the priests and religious sisters assigned to the home, to the volunteer group, to the cooperators, to the youth center, the students and professionals of the professional formation center, to the benefactors and to all those who in any way support the institution and come to the aid of its patients with exquisite human and Christian delicacy. May the Lord, who is identified with the weak, the sick, the suffering, with those who are put aside, always give you a taste of the joy of love and service, and prepare for you the reward and eternal promise of the Gospel. Continue with courage and care your civic and Christian duties of charity, fraternity, solidarity!

A TRIAL THAT IS ALSO A MYSTERY

2. But I am here especially to greet and embrace you, the suffering of all classes, little ones and adults, beloved brothers of the suffering Christ.

It is with a sincerely moved spirit that I approach you, and it is above all for you that I have come to this home.

I wish at this moment to express all the deep sympathy I feel for each one of you, all my understanding for the sickness you bear in your body and in your mind; I would like to speak with you individually to fill you with comfort and encouragement.

Your life as handicapped persons constitutes a great trial; a trial for you first of all, but a trial also for your parents, for those who love you, and for those who ask: Why this infirmity?

Truly, yours is a trial that is also a mystery.

I am thinking at this moment of Jesus, who, traveling the roads of Palestine, preferably approached, as only He could do, with His infinite human and divine compassion, the poor, the suffering, the sick in body and mind, and brought them all consolation, opened their heart to hope and sometimes even offered the gift of healing.

Today too it is only to Him that we must turn if we want to receive the light that reveals at least a little of the mystery of suffering, and the grace of being able to accept it patiently.

The Lord does not ask us to close our eyes to infirmity. It is very real, and we must have a clear awareness of it. He asks us to look more deeply, to believe that in these suffering bodies there throbs not only human life with all its dignity and rights, but also, by virtue of Baptism, divine life itself, the marvelous life of children of God. If to the external eyes of men you appear weak and infirm, before God you are great and brilliant in your being. Don Guanella called you "my pearls" and named you the "beloved of Providence."

There is yet another very important reality that Jesus reveals to us.

In the society of men, powerful and cultured people occupy first place and are most conspicuous; in the kingdom of God, though, the opposite happens: the first and the greatest—Jesus tells us—are the children, the weak, the poor, the suffering. God's way of doing things is really disconcerting for man. St. Paul the Apostle tells us, "God has chosen the weak in the world to confound the strong" (1 Cor. 1:27).

This truth, which leaves us stunned, becomes credible if we look at the example of Jesus Himself. Jesus was not content with opening to us the mystery of suffering. He gave us the most convincing answer by taking our infirmities upon Himself, becoming the Man of sorrows who knows suffering (cf. Is. 53:3).

When, therefore, we ask God, "Why does this innocent person have to suffer?" God in turn asks us a question: "Don't you see me present in your brother who is suffering? And what are you doing for me and for him?"

TRANSFORM YOUR "PASSION" THROUGH LOVE

3. Beloved! My pastoral visit, so near to Holy Week, thus becomes a meditation on the "passion of Christ" and on the "passion of Man." Reflecting on the Divine Word who goes through the anguish of Gethsemane and the agony of the cross to redeem man from the darkness of error and evil, we understand why mankind too must go through the Calvary of suffering. Until the second coming of Christ, the redemption is being accomplished, day by day. I welcome the opportunity to express my hearty congratulations for all the modern resources adopted to meet the needs of the sick, to develop their possibilities, to make them self-sufficient as much as can be hoped, caring for them and making them responsible; and at the same time I encourage and exhort you to make use of every physio- and psycho-therapeutic technology with care and good will. Yet I am urged also to remind you that despite all the conquests of science, the "passion of Christ," together with the "passion of Man," endures in history in the role and in the prospective of the final resurrection in Christ for all who have believed in Him and have loved and suffered with Him. Don Guanella, at the end of his life, in the throes of his final illness, one day uttered this expression: "Sin must be a great evil if it brought such terrible pain on earth." It was

the manifestation of his simple, but firm and sure faith that had made him discover the "hidden treasure" for which he had given up everything and which, before he died, still inspired in him the summary of his message: *Omnia in caritate!* (Everything in charity!) "Paradise, Paradise!"

You too, the sick, relatives and friends, transform your "passion" into an act of redemptive love; offer it every day and raise it to the Most High as the priest at the altar offers the pure and spotless Host and the cup of eternal salvation! May you be helped in this resolution by Blessed Luigi Guanella, who in the happiness of heaven always remains an alert guardian of his works, and especially in this home. May the motherly affection of the most holy Virgin, Mother of Providence, accompany you. Devotion to her must be preeminent in the program of your life and of your day. And may you also be sustained by my prayer, which I assure you from the bottom of my heart, while I impart my blessing to everyone.

Blessed Luigi Guanella's Vast Program of Charity

At the end of his visit to the Don Guanella Institution on Via Aurelia Antica, on March 28, 1982, Pope John Paul II met with the Servants of Charity and the Daughters of St. Mary of Providence, who staff the Don Guanella homes. Following is the prepared text of the address that the Holy Father decided to set aside in order to speak to the religious extemporaneously.

Dearest sons and daughters of Don Guanella,

1. Having completed the long tour of this city of love and pain, we are now gathered here for this brief but significant meeting reserved especially for you who have most closely followed the footsteps and the ideals of him who dedicated his whole life to loving and helping the suffering.

You, religious "Servants of Charity," and you sisters, "Daughters of St. Mary of Providence," who this year are celebrating the first centenary of your founding, must rejoice to be able to imitate the example of your blessed founder, continuing to carry out the works of charity inspired and initiated by him.

Don Guanella, from his boyhood, strongly felt this call to love the poor and abandoned. Ordained a priest in Como (May 26, 1866), he already had his very clear plan of work and apostolate. A man extremely sensitive to the condition of those who are set aside, of the handicapped, orphans, the elderly, invalids, of persons without home or affection, he wanted to be always and for everyone the Good Samaritan of the Gospel, and he dedicated his life completely to works of mercy. You well know how much he had to suffer to be able to realize this sublime torment of his. Intelligent, ingenious, industrious, rich in courage and generosity, with an intellectual training and a sure and solid asceticism, simple and of vast horizons, he was undoubtedly an extraordinary personality who, despite innumerable and continuous difficulties, oppositions, humiliations, persecutions, calumnies and suspicions, he succeeded, with his tenacious and total confidence in God, in carrying out his vast and heroic program of charity.

2. In the address at his beatification, Paul VI stated that "the adventurous, complicated and feverish experiences of the prodigious life" of this man of God were always sustained by a "great piety, assiduous prayer, a striving for continuous communion with God" *(Insegnamenti di Paolo VI*, Vol. II, 1964, pp. 611f.). He wanted to be only a faithful servant, a manifestation of divine goodness, a sign of divine Providence. From this arose his apostolic anxiety, first as a priest in care of souls, then, from 1882 onward, as founder and builder of homes and centers for the care of the most emarginated, beginning with Pianello Lario and then in Como, and subsequently in other areas of the diocese, in Italy, in Rome, in America. Consoler of the afflicted, he used to say to you spiritual sons and daughters of his, and he still says: "The whole world is your homeland.... You cannot stop so long as there are

poor to be cared for and needy to be provided for." And he used to add: "It is not enough to relieve misery, you must go find it." But he also emphasized that "the soul and secret of the work is confidence in the Lord." Paul VI exclaimed with burning enthusiasm: "The work of Don Guanella is the work of God! And if it is the work of God, it is marvelous, it is beneficial, it is holy!" *(Insegnamenti, ibid.)*

3. We must listen to and accept the message of the saints! They, especially enlightened by the Most High, with their life and their intuitions, are the answer to our questions and our problems. From the saints we can understand that the one thing that counts is the love of God for men and vice versa, and that in particular, they build up the history of the Church and live it day by day, embodying before the world the teaching of the Gospel. The specific message that Don Guanella left is that of God's "paternity," that is, His love, His Providence, His affection and mercy present in the vicissitudes of men. "It is God who does it. Everything is of God," he used to state, "even if the Lord wants everything down here to follow common ways." "How can God not think of what He has willed?" And making use of all the devices and means of foresight and human providence, Don Guanella was convinced that to be authentic "Servants of Charity" means to be above all and always "Servants of Truth." For this reason we do not find empty rhetoric in him: he prayed and he acted; he caused to pray and he caused to act! Firm in the perennial doctrine of the Church, faithful to the solemn Magisterium

of Pius IX, Leo XIII, and Pius X, his great friend, he passed unharmed through the insidious storm of positivism, rationalism, modernism; he was a writer and a clear and persuasive apologist, and in that very era, buffeted by terrible pains and marked by so many tears, he wanted to be a concrete and living proof of God's love. Darkness exists only that light may shine; evil and pain remain in human history only that everyone may love, feeling nostalgia for God and a happy eternity! So he used to say, "They want us in everything as victims, they want us especially as victims conformed to the great Victim of Calvary, to raise up towers of salvation for souls." A servant of truth in order to be truly a servant of charity, Don Guanella understood that in order to love in a concrete and effective way, it was necessary to focus on the Eucharist and the anticipation of eternal life. So he exhorted his sisters, "You need not list the hardships of life, illness and death! Make yourselves victims for God and for the work of God...." "You must decay in prayer and concealment, like the grain that gives bread to everybody."

It is certainly an austere and sometimes heroic message, this message of Blessed Luigi Guanella; it is also as relevant as ever. Divine goodness wants to be present and visible today too, through our love: this is the charge that Don Guanella has left.

4. I entrust to the most holy Virgin, to the "Madonna of Work," as she was invoked by him, your intentions, your works, all your fellow brothers and sisters scattered throughout the

world, and especially vocations to your two congregations. May they always be chosen and numerous in order to continue with courage and confidence the witness of God's love in the world. May the intercessory apostolic blessing accompany and comfort you.

Fostering the Role of the Elderly in the Family and in Society

On April 29, 1982, the Holy Father received in audience over three thousand members of the National Federation of the Elderly in Commerce and Tourism. Following is the text of the address given by John Paul II to the pilgrims.

1. I am happy to have this meeting with you, men and women of the National Federation of the Elderly in Commerce and Tourism during this year in which, besides the usual touristic-cultural manifestation represented by your "month," you are celebrating at the same time the year of the elderly.

I greet you one and all, and I thank you from my heart for your visit.

2. The joy of being in the presence of such a large group, which moreover belongs to a much larger organization, grows upon examination of your program and aims, which are primarily of a social nature, directed towards enhancing the role of the elderly, improving their living conditions, and reintegrating them into the family and society.

It is for me a reason for satisfaction and hope to learn that your organization not only maintains a relationship of close collaboration with the Christian workers' movement, present at this audience with a significant number of representatives, but above all that it is guided in its multiple social welfare activities by moral and religious principles, and recognizes Christianity and the Catholic Church as being the point of reference and surest means of support for the increase of man's dignity.

For this reason I wish to reflect with you upon two recent documents which closely relate to your programs, the Encyclical *Laborem exercens* and the Apostolic Exhortation *Familiaris consortio,* so that you will study them more deeply.

3. You are now, or have been, men and women of work. You have spent the best energies of your lives, dedicating them to the growth of your dignity and of your humanity, at your workbenches in the multiple occupations in the commercial and tourist sectors. And now, even if your federation carries the official title of "elderly," the circle of your activity cannot be considered closed for this reason.

The theme presented for our consideration is not of small importance, and it touches one of the vital, often dramatic, points in today's society. It is a fundamental problem: that of being employed. It is a problem which becomes particularly painful when it affects young people, with all the consequences that arise in the economic and social development of the community. But under certain aspects it is also a problem which affects the elderly who, having reached an age limit, must on the one hand give up their places to the younger work force. On the other hand, however, they cannot lock themselves away in the corner of forced inactivity while they are still capable of making a valid contribution. This would be doubly harmful, both from the human and social points of view. The community cannot deprive itself of the wealth of its older members' experience, just as the elderly cannot and must not impoverish their humanity.

As I wrote in *Laborem exercens*, work is one of man's goods, it is a good of his humanity since also through work man "fulfills himself as a man and even, in a certain sense, becomes more man" (no. 9). Indeed, one can grow in humanity, can be more, at any age.

In this perspective, in your organization likewise, new horizons and much wider fields are opening up, taking advantage of possibilities for activity which exist on the national and local levels, and opening up new ones in a creative sense, always keeping in mind human advancement under the double profile of ongoing education and service to the community, giving new impulse to various types of volunteer work. There are many sectors being discovered in which elderly people could be placed, doing work appropriate to their age and experience. The result would be of enormous advantage and benefit to everyone, both to the individual and to the community.

4. The second problem concerns full integration of the elderly into the circle of family life. In the Apostolic Exhortation *Familiaris consortio*, I wrote in this regard: "There are cultures which manifest a unique veneration and great love for the elderly." They "continue to be present and to take an active and responsible part in family life, though having to respect the autonomy of the new family; above all they carry out the important mission of being a witness to the past and a source of wisdom for the young and for the future. Other cultures, however, especially in the wake of disordered industrial and urban development, have both in the past and in the present set the elderly aside in unacceptable ways. This causes acute suffering to them and spiritually impoverishes many families."

This problem is of growing seriousness and relevance to the present day, both because in the most industrialized and urbanized examples of modern society signs are not lacking of a disturbing degradation of fundamental family values, and because the number of elderly is increasing.

When a society, allowing itself to be guided solely by the criteria of consumption and efficiency, divides men into active and inactive and considers the inactive as second-class citizens, abandoning them to loneliness, it cannot be called a truly civilized society. When a family does not wish to have in the house their own blood relatives, the very young and the elderly, children and old people, and one neglects the other in some way or manner, it certainly does not deserve being called a loving community.

It is necessary to reconstruct the image of the family as a community of persons in which, in the light of the Gospel message, the members of every age live together in respect for everyone's rights: the rights of women, children and the elderly. It is necessary to rebuild the family as a more thorough and richer school for humanity, in the communion of persons, in the sharing of joys and suffering.

5. I know that your organization tries hard to take inspiration in its commitment from the value of the Gospel, without which the vital problems I have mentioned and which touch such a large category of persons could not be adequately resolved.

I urge you to work with ever more generous dedication so that the Christian principles from which your endeavors draw strength may become known, deepened and put into practice.

May my blessing, which I extend from my heart to all your loved ones and to all the persons to whom your concerns are directed, accompany you.

Suffering Can Enrich the Individual and the Whole Church

After meeting Queen Elizabeth II at Buckingham Palace on May 28, 1982, the Holy Father presided at a para-liturgical ceremony for the sick in Southwark Cathedral. During the long and moving meeting with the sick, the Pope gave the following discourse.

My brothers and sisters,

1. Praised be Jesus Christ! Praised be Jesus Christ who invites us to share in His life through our Baptism. Praised be Jesus Christ who calls us *to unite our sufferings to His* so that we may be one with Him in giving glory to the Father in heaven.

Today I greet you in the name of Jesus. I thank all of you for the welcome you have given me. I want you to know how I have looked forward to this meeting with you, especially with those of you who are sick, disabled or infirm. I myself have had a share in suffering, and I have known the physical weakness that comes with injury and sickness.

2. It is precisely because I have experienced suffering that I am able to affirm with ever greater conviction what St. Paul says in the second reading: "Neither death, nor life, nor angels, nor principalities, nor things present, nor things to come, nor powers, nor height, nor depth, nor anything else in all creation, will be able to separate us from the love of God in Christ Jesus our Lord" (Rom. 8:38-39).

Dear friends, there is no force or power that can block God's love for you. Sickness and suffering seem to contradict all that is worthy, all that is desired by man. And yet no disease, no injury, no infirmity can ever deprive you of your dignity as children of God, as brothers and sisters of Jesus Christ.

3. By His dying on the cross, Christ shows us how to make sense of our suffering. In His passion we find the inspiration and strength to turn away from any temptation to resentment, and grow through pain into new life.

Suffering is an invitation to be more like the Son in doing the Father's will. It offers us an opportunity to imitate Christ who died to redeem mankind from sin. Thus the Father has disposed that suffering can enrich the individual and the whole Church.

4. We acknowledge that the Anointing of the Sick is for the benefit of the whole person. We find this point demonstrated in the liturgical texts of the sacramental celebration: "Make this oil a remedy for all who are anointed with it; heal them in body, in soul and in spirit, and deliver them from every affliction."

The anointing is therefore a source of strength for both the soul and the body. The prayer of the Church asks that sin and the remnants of sin be taken away (cf. DS 1969). It also implores a restoration of health, but always in order that bodily healing may bring greater union with God through the increase of grace.

In her teaching on this sacrament, the Church passes on the truth contained in our first reading from St. James: "Is any among you sick? Let him call for the elders of the Church and let them pray over him, anointing him with oil in the name of the Lord; and the prayer of faith will save the sick man, and the Lord will raise him up; and if he has committed sins, he will be forgiven" (Jas. 5:14-15).

5. This sacrament should be approached in a spirit of great confidence, like the leper in the Gospel that has just been proclaimed. Even the desperateness of the man's condition did not stop him from approaching Jesus with trust. *We too must believe in Christ's healing love and reaffirm that nothing will separate us from that love.* Surely Jesus wishes to say: "I will it; be clean" (Mt. 8:3); be healed; be strong; be saved.

My dear brothers and sisters, as you live the passion of Christ you strengthen the Church by the witness of your faith. You proclaim by your patience, your endurance and your joy the mystery of Christ's redeeming power. *You will find the crucified Lord in the midst of your sickness and suffering.*

6. As Veronica ministered to Christ on His way to Calvary, so Christians have accepted the care of those in pain and sorrow as privileged opportunities to minister to Christ Himself. I commend and bless all those who work for the sick in hospitals, residential homes and centers of care for the dying. I would like to say to you doctors, nurses, chaplains and all other hospital staff: Yours is a noble vocation. *Remember it is Christ to whom you minister in the sufferings of your brothers and sisters.*

7. I support with all my heart those who recognize and defend the law of God which governs human life. We must never forget that every person, from the moment of conception to the last breath, is a unique child of God and has a right to life. This right should be defended by the attentive care of the medical and nursing professions and by the protection of the law. Every human life is willed by our heavenly Father and is a part of His loving plan.

No state has the right to contradict moral values which are rooted in the nature of man himself. These values are the precious heritage of civilization. If society begins to deny the worth of any individual or to subordinate the human person to pragmatic or utilitarian considerations, it begins to destroy the defenses that safeguard its own fundamental values.

8. Today I make an urgent plea to this nation. Do not neglect your sick and elderly. Do not turn away from the handicapped and the dying. Do not push them to the margins of society. For if you do, you will fail to understand that they represent an important truth. The sick, the elderly, the handicapped and the dying teach us that weakness is a creative part of human living, and that suffering can be embraced with no loss of dignity. Without the presence of these people in your midst you might be tempted to think of health, strength and power as the only important values to be pursued in life. *But the wisdom of Christ and the power of Christ are to be seen in the weakness of those who share His sufferings.*

Let us keep the sick and the handicapped at the center of our lives. Let us treasure them and recognize with gratitude the debt we owe them. We begin by imagining that we are giving to them; we end by realizing that they have enriched us.

May God bless and comfort all who suffer. And may Jesus Christ, the Savior of the world and Healer of the sick, make His light shine through human weakness as a beacon for us and for all mankind. Amen.

My dear brothers and sisters in Christ, as we speak of suffering, affliction and death, we cannot forget those who have suffered and died during the armed conflict in the South Atlantic. Let us now remember in our prayers the victims of both sides. May the Father of mercies and of all consolation be close to the wounded and to all the families touched by tragedy.

May He give eternal rest to those who have died in Christ and to those who mourn in Christian hope, and let us pray that negotiations may pave the way to a just and lasting peace. We ask this through Christ our Lord. Amen.

Assisting the Handicapped Is a Sign of Communion

Before leaving Edinburgh for Glasgow, the Holy Father made a brief visit to St. Joseph's Hospital of Rosewell on June 1, 1982, where he spoke to the handicapped children and their assistants as follows.

My dear friends and children in Jesus Christ,

1. I am delighted to be making this visit to St. Joseph's Hospital, Rosewell, and I have come

for several reasons. First, to greet you, the patients in the care of the hospital, suffering from both mental and physical handicap, and also the Sisters of Charity of St. Vincent de Paul who administer the hospital, with the medical advisers, nursing and auxiliary staff, chaplains and voluntary workers for the handicapped in general, and the parents and families of those who are receiving this special care.

Another reason for my visit is to bear witness to the Church's mission from Christ to care for all God's people, especially those most in need. I was interested to learn that the ancient Gaelic language of Scotland has a most telling phrase, *corramaich fo chùram Dhè*, which speaks of the handicapped as living under God's protection—"God's handicapped." Such a sensitive description, or title, captures a whole variety of profoundly Christian insights into the meaning of life and its dignity, a life which all of us have received from the Creator and whose course we share in various ways as separate individuals. And what is more, for the baptized this is a new life of grace in and through Jesus Christ, the Savior of the world.

2. Those who do not enjoy the fullness of what is called a normal way of life, through either mental or serious physical handicap, are often compensated in part by qualities which people often take for granted or even distort, under the influence of a materialistic society: such things as a radiant love—transparent, innocent and yearning—and the attraction of loving and selfless care. In this regard, we often find in the Gos-

pels the refreshing example of Jesus Himself, and the loving bond of affection between Him and the sick or disabled: how many were His exertions for them, the great words of faith addressed to them, and His wonderful interventions on their behalf, "for power came forth from him" (Lk. 6:19; cf. Mk. 1:32-34). There were times when He went out of His way to identify Himself with the sick and the suffering, He who was to suffer such a passion and death Himself: "I was sick and you visited me.... As you did it to one of the least of these my brethren, you did it to me" (Mt. 25:36, 40).

3. These latter words of Jesus are also a source of great consolation to all those who care for the sick and disabled: nurses and medical staff, sisters and chaplains, parents, voluntary helpers and friends. For your loving care and self-sacrifice are all too often a source of your own suffering, through tiredness, emotional and mental strain, and other such burdens. So much so that, when you identify with the handicapped in your loving and attentive service to them, you also share the accolade of St. Paul: "In my flesh I make up what is lacking in Christ's afflictions for the sake of his body, that is, the church" (Col. 1:24; cf. 2 Cor. 1:5, 12:19). And when you really feel at your lowest ebb, our Lord Himself has a further and very personal message of comfort: "Come to me, all who labor and are heavy-laden, and I will give you rest. Take my yoke upon you, and learn from me; for I am gentle and lowly in heart, and you will find rest for your souls. For my yoke is easy, and my burden is light" (Mt.

11:28-30). These words of encouragement from Christ, which I pass on to you in His name, are meant also for those who are caring for the handicapped at home, and trying to give them as normal a family life as possible.

4. I know from Cardinal Gray that this Archdiocese of St. Andrew's and Edinburgh, as well as other dioceses in Scotland, provides a reassuring and supportive role through special Masses and reunions for the handicapped and their helpers at regular intervals in various parish centers. In this spirit of Christian cooperation and service, you are admirably obeying the call to rejoice with those who rejoice and to suffer with those who suffer (cf. Rom. 12:15). This offers not only a stimulus to a truly human and humanizing disposition, but also a sign of communion that enriches both the one who gives and the one who receives.

5. No visit to Rosewell would be complete without mentioning a young woman whose holy life and final suffering gave full expression to the message from Sacred Scripture that we have reflected on this morning: *the Venerable Margaret Sinclair*, known later in the religious life as Sister Mary Francis of the Five Wounds, Poor Clare Colletine, who lived from 1900 until 1925. For it was to Rosewell that Margaret came on holidays with other members of her family from their home in Edinburgh. Margaret could well be described as one of God's little ones who, through her very simplicity, was touched by God with the strength of real holiness of life, whether as a child, a young woman, an apprentice, a

factory-worker, member of a trade union, or a professed sister in religion. How appropriate it is, then, that Rosewell should be chosen for the location of the Margaret Sinclair Center, the purpose of which is to make her inspiring example better known and to promote her cause for beatification. I fully appreciate the aspirations of the Catholics of Scotland and elsewhere for that singular event to be realized, and I know that you are praying that it may come about.

With this recollection of the Venerable Margaret Sinclair, I leave you with her inspiration. In drawing us to love and assist the handicapped, the Lord Jesus touches our lives with His strength, and finally rewards us according to His promise: "As you did it to one of the least of these my brethren, you did it to me" (Mt. 25:40).

Praised be Jesus Christ!

Commitment to Life Is Urgent

On June 8, 1982, Pope John Paul II visited Bambino Gesù Children's Hospital to bless and inaugurate the new medical-surgical center for pediatric cardiology, and gave the following address.

Distinguished ladies and gentlemen,
My dear brothers and sisters,

1. Once again I have come, filled with emotion, to visit the Bambino Gesù Pediatric Hospital. I willingly accepted the administration's invitation to bless and inaugurate the new Medical-Surgical Department of Pediatric Cardiology, and I would like to give public expression today to my satisfaction and pleasure at the fact

that this hospital is continually renewing itself and adding a complex of advanced apparatus, with the aim of being able to offer the little heart patients the most suitable and exact treatment which will give them back their longed-for health.

I feel it my duty on this occasion to express my sincere thanks to all those who thought of, decided on and planned this marvelous scientific complex, and all those who have generously and unselfishly contributed to its realization, and to all those professors, doctors, the paramedic staff and sisters who carry out their duties with such praiseworthy devotion.

But I have come to this place especially because I was called here at the instance of the thin, agonized cry of these children who bear in their fragile little bodies the weight of sickness and suffering, and I want to tell them and show them, in your name, in the name of their parents, in the name of the Church, all the enormous affection with which we want to surround them, particularly in the times of their most acute weakness.

WE SHARE IN THE SUFFERING OF JESUS

2. Visiting a hospital, and a children's hospital in particular, arouses in the depths of one's heart some of the most radical questions about the meaning of life and man's existence: the continuous, incessant, inescapable presence of suffering, especially that of the "innocent," strikes the astonished and perplexed human

reason as a genuine "scandal" capable of bringing into question and into dangerous crises the certainties on which our intellectual, religious and ethical lives are based. The heartfelt whimpering and the piercing crying of a suffering child can seem almost a protest by the whole of humanity against the impenetrable silence of God, who permits such an amount of suffering.

Where human reason seems to come up against a thick wall of shadow and considers itself right in assuming an attitude of revolt, the divine Word introduces us into the "mystery" of human suffering, presenting to our consideration and our experience Jesus, Christ and Lord, the Son of God, in whom the prophetic figure of the "Suffering Servant" and "Man of Sorrows" (Is. 53:3) takes flesh: Jesus, who is so deeply moved in the face of others' suffering, who takes on suffering completely in His passion and death —the obligatory passage for His resurrection and glorification.

Well then, if we suffer, we share in the sufferings of Jesus, in order, as St. Paul will tell us, that we may also share in His glory (cf. Rom. 8:17). If we carry always and everywhere in our body the sufferings and death of Jesus, it is so that the life of Jesus may also be manifested in our body (cf. 2 Cor. 4:10). And the same Apostle, who in his life experienced a long apprenticeship in pain, can speak of the joy which he feels in the sufferings that he endures, because he can complete in his flesh what is lacking in the sufferings of Christ, for the sake of His Body which is the Church (cf. Col. 1:24).

In this Christian view of pain, the lament and crying of those who suffer, especially children, are not therefore a bitter protest, but a solemn, pure and stirring prayer of entreaty which is raised from this poor earth to the throne of God, that all men may be freed and purified from evil, that they may order their lives in harmony with the demands of divine revelation and may show themselves genuine "children of God."

BLESSED ARE YOU

3. From this point of view, Jesus declared "blessed" those who mourn and are afflicted, for they will be comforted (cf. Mt. 5:4); and on the day of His return in glory as supreme and final Judge of history, He will identify Himself with all the suffering of the earth: "...I was sick and you visited me.... As you did it to one of the least of these my brethren, you did it to me" (cf. Mt. 25:36, 40). This solemn proclamation from the lips of Christ must give a new and supernatural meaning to the task which you all perform on behalf of the least of the brethren of Jesus, the children who are sick and suffering. Your specific competence, your exemplary devotion, your generous commitment are directed towards Jesus, the God-Man, who is mysteriously present in them. It is in this spirit of the Gospel that your profession, in itself worthy of the greatest respect, becomes an authentic "mission" of faith and a contribution to the total elevation of man, made in the image and likeness of God.

From this place of suffering, but also of hope, I would like to address an invitation, an appeal, to scientists and those in whose hands is the fate of the earthly city: it is urgent, it is necessary, that enterprises, studies, research and contributions be directed and coordinated towards the alleviation of the suffering of our brethren who have been struck by various calamities and are the victims of illness. It is necessary to provide the proper finance for these studies and researches geared to the physical health of citizens. Let not the largest expenditure of the various countries be for armaments, the most sophisticated instruments capable only of causing destruction, death and desperation, while on the other hand no attention is given to those works and initiatives which are necessary and cannot be deferred if the life of men, even from a health point of view, is to be spent quietly and serenely in peace, justice and order.

It is my wish that this pediatric hospital, the Bambino Gesù, will be a forward-pointing sign and a center for studies in which these little children will be offered, along with the ever more advanced treatments which technology and science can provide, the most sensitive affection and devotion, inspired by the message of love of the Gospel of Christ.

With these wishes and in this spirit, I wholeheartedly confer my apostolic blessing upon these dear patients, the members of their families, the administration, the doctors, the paramedic staff, the sisters, the friends of the Bambino Gesù and all here present.

Assure the Respect of the Human Person

During the course of his visit to the headquarters of the International Committee of the Red Cross on June 15, 1982, the Holy Father addressed the following remarks to those present.

Mr. President,
Ladies and gentlemen,

1. I thank you sincerely for the statements you have just made concerning the Holy See's action and my efforts. I have been very attentive to all that you said about my homeland, about El Salvador, the Middle East, Lebanon, about peace in general, since they are situations which are of deep concern to the Catholics I represent and which are always very much present in my prayers.

2. It is a great joy for me to greet, at the very seat of the International Committee of the Red Cross, the competent representatives of an organization to whom humanity is greatly indebted! In fact, from its foundation through the efforts of Henri Dunant more than a century ago now, this institution which sprang up in the hearts of some generous Swiss citizens has met an echo in the entire world, for which it can rightly rejoice.

And through you the Pope is pleased in his turn to render a warm homage to all those men and women of good will who, within the structure of the Red Cross, have had no other ambition than to serve, for humanity, their brothers and sisters who suffer because of the inhumanity of other men, from absurd conflicts or from natural disasters.

On the other hand, who would not subscribe to the fundamental principles of the Red Cross, adopted on the occasion of its twentieth congress, and in a special way to the commitment to "protect life" and to "assure the respect of the human person" without any discrimination, to encourage "mutual understanding, friendship, cooperation and a lasting peace among all peoples"?

ADMIRABLE WORK OF THE RED CROSS ORGANIZATION

3. Without doubt the same spirit which animated the founder of the Red Cross and his first collaborators prohibits me from emphasizing at too great length the benefits which are due to the International Committee of the Red Cross. And I am thinking obviously also of the admirable work of the national organizations of the Red Cross, as well as their federation or international league. The Red Cross has brought this aid, in the midst of many wars and many calamities, to the civilian and military victims of armed conflicts, to the wounded or ill on all sides, as well as to refugees, prisoners, and separated families, especially during this period in Lebanon. That spirit is one of abnegation, which can find its own compensation in the knowledge of the service rendered, in the dedication which often does not hesitate in the face of the supreme sacrifice, and

which often enough is manifested in the execution of unknown but very necessary tasks!

Fulfilling its mission of aid, care and comfort, giving the necessary stimulus and support to local initiatives, remaining faithful to the proposition of neutrality which characterized the originating insight of the founders, proposing with respect but with tenacity its intervention at the very heart of conflicts, the Red Cross has acquired a moral authority throughout the entire world, inasmuch as the effectiveness of your action is not limited to the multiplicity of services rendered to alleviate all the physical and moral suffering encountered, but because the understanding which the warring sides and the public authorities must usually witness to your mission —as regards conventions—means for your moral duties which widen the field in which your responsibility is exercised in nations and international organizations. Yes, you contribute to the development of international humanitarian rights, whose field of application you continuously seek to broaden.

INSTILLING RESPECT FOR BASIC RIGHTS

4. In this respect, in the sphere of the rights of man, allow me to once more insist upon the subject of torture and other inhuman treatment. The governments which subscribe to the Four Geneva Conventions are, on the other hand, committed to forbidding such treatments and to authorize the delegates of the Red Cross to visit

those who are interned and to meet with the prisoners without witnesses. I hope that, also on this point, your missions are accepted in all countries in order to banish this bloody plague from humanity. In this way, with your specific means, you contribute to instilling respect for the basic rights of man and his dignity, bringing together, without distinctions on the other hand, all those who, believers or nonbelievers, are enamored of these ideals.

5. In this service to man, Christians easily arrive at the aims and the practice of the Red Cross. They find in their faith a stimulus and additional motivations for seeing in a wounded, degraded or poverty-stricken person a neighbor to love and to help, whoever he may be. Indeed, they find in him the very image of the Christ who identified Himself with the prisoner, with the ill, with the stranger, with the man deprived of everything. How many pages of the Gospel take on in this case striking emphasis, beginning with the parable of the Good Samaritan! And with regard to torture, the Christian from his childhood is placed before the story of the passion of Christ. The memory of Jesus, stripped, beaten, scorned even up to the sufferings of His agony, should always make him refuse to see similar treatment applied to one of his brothers in humanity. Spontaneously, Christ's disciple refuses every recourse to such methods which nothing could justify and in which the dignity of man is as much debased in his torturer as in the torturer's victim.

WISH TO COLLABORATE

6. The Catholic Church, on her part, meets willingly with your organizations. During the last two world wars, for example, a cooperative effort took place between the initiatives of the Red Cross and those of Catholic charity organizations. Such collaboration has continued to aid populations starved by wars or victims of natural disaster. Among the various works supported by the Church and the International Committee of the Red Cross and the Societies of the Red Cross, important relations have already been established in the field, and I am happy that the Holy See and the International Committee of the Red Cross are examining more ways of collaborating in activities in favor of peace.

7. Finally, in order to achieve the goals it has set for itself, the Red Cross must be guaranteed respect for the international conventions and protocols given them by the various states and by the authorities whose task it is to apply wise measures. With you, I address an urgent appeal that the humanitarian laws contained in these conventions be sincerely and scrupulously observed, and that, if necessary, they be completed by international instruments against inhuman treatment and torture in particular. They could furnish serious guarantees for the physical and psychological protection of victims and for the respect due them. Every man everywhere should be able to depend upon such guarantees. And it is the duty of every state concerned about the well-being of its own citizens to

underwrite these guarantees and to have the courage to put them into effect.

8. Happy to have been able to express to you my esteem and my encouragement to continue the work you have undertaken, I pray God, the God who is "rich in mercy," to bless all those who, in the service of the Red Cross, according to the standard of Christian charity, can show the persons they find in difficulties, and can stir up in their encounters, a respect and a dedication which humanize our tormented and shattered world. And I pray that He will inspire such feelings in an ever-growing number of our contemporaries. May humanity heed even more that appeal which deeply touched Henri Dunant: "We are all brothers!"

Daughters of St. Paul

IN MASSACHUSETTS
50 St. Paul's Ave., Jamaica Plain, Boston, MA 02130; **617-522-8911; 617-522-0875**
172 Tremont Street, Boston, MA 02111; **617-426-5464; 617-426-4230**
IN NEW YORK
78 Fort Place, Staten Island, NY 10301; **212-447-5071**
59 East 43rd Street, New York, NY 10017; **212-986-7580**
625 East 187th Street, Bronx, NY 10458; **212-584-0440**
525 Main Street, Buffalo, NY 14203; **716-847-6044**
IN NEW JERSEY
Hudson Mall — Route 440 and Communipaw Ave., Jersey City, NJ 07304; **201-433-7740**
IN CONNECTICUT
202 Fairfield Ave., Bridgeport, CT 06604; **203-335-9913**
IN OHIO
2105 Ontario St. (at Prospect Ave.), Cleveland, OH 44115; **216-621-9427**
25 E. Eighth Street, Cincinnati, OH 45202; **513-721-4838**
IN PENNSYLVANIA
1719 Chestnut Street, Philadelphia, PA 19103; **215-568-2638**
IN VIRGINIA
1025 King St., Alexandria, VA 22314 **703-683-1741**
IN FLORIDA
2700 Biscayne Blvd., Miami, FL 33137; **305-573-1618**
IN LOUISIANA
4403 Veterans Memorial Blvd., Metairie, LA 70002; **504-887-7631; 504-007-0113**
1800 South Acadian Thruway, P.O. Box 2028, Baton Rouge, LA 70821 **504-343-4057; 504-343-3814**
IN MISSOURI
1001 Pine Street (at North 10th), St. Louis, MO 63101; **314-621-0346; 314-231-1034**
IN ILLINOIS
172 North Michigan Ave., Chicago, IL 60601; **312-346-4228 312-346-3240**
IN TEXAS
114 Main Plaza, San Antonio, TX 78205; **512-224-8101**
IN CALIFORNIA
1570 Fifth Avenue, San Diego, CA 92101; **714-232-1442**
46 Geary Street, San Francisco, CA 94108; **415-781-5180**
IN HAWAII
1143 Bishop Street, Honolulu, HI 96813; **808-521-2731**
IN ALASKA
750 West 5th Avenue, Anchorage AK 99501; **907-272-8183**

IN CANADA
3022 Dufferin Street, Toronto 395, Ontario, Canada
IN ENGLAND
128, Notting Hill Gate, London W11 3QG, England
133 Corporation Street, Birmingham B4 6PH, England
5A-7 Royal Exchange Square, Glasgow G1 3AH, England
82 Bold Street, Liverpool L1 4HR, England
IN AUSTRALIA
58 Abbotsford Rd., Homebush, N.S.W., Sydney 2140, Australia